What Do You Do
After
You Plug It In?

William Barden, Jr. is currently a full-time technical writer and consultant, specializing in small computer systems. He has 20 years experience in computer programming, computer systems analysis, and computer design. Mr. Barden is a member of the Associates for Computing Machinery and the IEEE. His major interest is home computing but he still finds time to devote to his other interests of amateur radio, mathematical games, and sailing.

Mr. Barden's other books include *How To Program Microcomputers, Microcomputers for Business Applications, Z-80 Microcomputer Handbook, Z-80 Microcomputer Design Projects, Guidebook to Small Computers,* and *Microcomputer Math,* all published by Howard W. Sams & Co., Inc.

WHAT DO YOU DO AFTER YOU PLUG IT IN?

by

William Barden, Jr.

Howard W. Sams & Co., Inc.
4300 WEST 62ND ST. INDIANAPOLIS, INDIANA 46268 USA

International Standard Book Number: 0-672-22008-3
Library of Congress Catalog Card Number: 82-62199

Edited by: *Arlet Pryor*

Printed in the United States of America.

Preface

Oh, oh! You didn't really believe that computer salesman, did you? Weren't you suspicious when he told you that you'd make a million in gold by running your VisiGold program? Didn't you think there was more to the story when he told you that computers never fail and would never need repair? How *could* you believe that you'd be writing programs to translate ancient Greek into Texas dialect in just two weeks?

Well, you've got the system now. There's no turning back. . . . To give you some help from this point though, I've written this guide. It will help you overcome some of the hurdles that you will encounter "after plugging the system in." It will answer some of the questions about writing and buying computer software, using data communications, getting service for your equipment when it fails, and using your systems for such exotic tasks as voice synthesis and control of your lawn sprinklers.

Computers aren't all powerful. As a matter of fact, sometimes they're just dumb! We've tried to give you the actual facts in this book, without a lot of hype and puffery that you might get from a computer manufacturer or salesperson. Computers can be a boon . . . if you know a few of the basic answers. This book tries to provide those answers.

What Do You Do After You Plug It In? is divided into three sections.

Section I describes *hardware*. What is available and what options you have.

The first chapter covers some of the basic things you should look for in a system for your application. The next chapter discusses *16-bit* microcomputers. Are they really as good as the manufacturers promise? Maybe not.

Chapter 3 describes *mass storage* devices, such as semiconductor memory, cassette tape, and disk, and compares the relative costs and problems.

Chapter 4 discusses one of the most costly *peripheral devices* of a microcomputer system, the system line printer. Which type is best? What should you watch out for when purchasing one. Why is a serial version of a printer sometimes a bad buy?

Chapter 5 describes high-resolution graphics, a computer option that enables you to draw shapes and figures in fine detail. Is it really necessary to go into such fine detail? I've gone into fine detail to let you know.

Other system devices such as plotters, digitizers, light pens, and clocks are described in the next chapter. These devices are excellent buys . . . and may even be useful.

The next section describes software. This is the most misunderstood area of small computer systems for a new user and can wind up costing the most money and grief.

Chapter 7 describes computer languages from *machine-language* to *high-level languages*. How do you talk to a computer? Which language is best?

The next chapter covers one of the most important elements of any computer with a disk capability, the software *operating system*. Operating systems are an excellent way to make your system easier to use.

Chapter 9 talks about how you can develop your own software. Is it really possible? How much time will it take to learn a language? I'll tell you how here.

Chapter 10 gives you tips on buying software. It's entirely possible to have 100 diskettes full of useless software. What are the secrets to making wise selections?

Section III contains information about applications and procedures.

Chapter 11 discusses disk files and how to use them. Disk files can be very powerful but also can be a mysterious element of computer systems. They're really not that difficult.

The next chapter describes *backup procedures*, one of the most important procedures you can perform to protect your disk files and data.

Chapters 13 and 14 describe basic elements of data communications and show you how you can connect your computer system to hundreds of data communications networks across the country, providing a huge *data base* of information.

Chapter 15 describes *speech synthesis* and *voice recognition* techniques. It's possible to teach your system to talk, but you'll have difficulty in making it listen!

The last chapter discusses ways in which you can let your computer control such "real-world" things as lights and lawn sprinklers and monitor temperature and other conditions.

Computers can be controlled, once you have some answers. I can't promise you a fortune in gold, but I'll provide some of the answers.

WILLIAM BARDEN, JR.

To Fred Blechman for his support

CONTENTS

Section 1: Hardware—What Is Available and Options

CHAPTER 1

CHAPTER 2

CHAPTER 3

CHAPTER 4

CHAPTER 5

CHAPTER 6

Section 2: Software—Existing Tools and Writing Your Own

CHAPTER 7

CHAPTER 8

CHAPTER 9

CHAPTER 10

Section 3: Applications and Procedures

CHAPTER 11

CHAPTER 12

Hardware — What Is Available and Options

Choosing Your System

Radio Shack TRS-80® Model III and Color Computer, Commodore 64 and VIC-20™, Apple® II and III, Texas Instruments TI-99/A, Sinclair ZX-81, Atari® 400™ and 800™, IBM Personal Computer, Hewlett-Packard HP-87, Osborne 1, and dozens of others! With so many small computers, how do you make an intelligent choice about which one to get? In this first chapter, you will find some rough guidelines about how to choose a small computer system that avoids the hype and puffery that accompany most advertisements and promotional spots for small computers. And, you will find the strengths and weaknesses of small computer systems, based on the application.

In spite of the blurbs and celebrity advertising spots from manufacturers, no one system will outperform all others. Most systems are more similar than different.

Some systems, however, are suited to perform certain types of applications better than others, so the question really becomes, "Which system is best for my application?"

Let us roughly divide the applications for your small computer into seven areas:

- Small business user—a computer for a company of up to 50 employees
- Smaller business user—a small operation of a dozen or fewer employees

- Professional user—essentially a one-person operation or very small business
- Entrepreneur user—you would like a system that will help you "play the market," make intelligent decisions about personal investments, and the like
- Household user—you would like a small system around the house for a variety of uses—balancing the checkbook, letting the kids do programmed instruction courses and games, and possibly even controlling the sprinkling systems
- Games player—you are tired of your children sticking quarters into *Urpman* (or losing money yourself!) and would like to buy your own system, primarily for games
- Upward-mobile, expensive toy user—you do not know much about computers, but they must be good—everyone on the block is talking about them, and you do not want to miss out!

You will notice larger businesses were left out. This does not mean that small computers are not suited to large businesses. One major company close to us recently bought 100 IBM Personal Computer Systems, and the IBM PC is definitely a small computer in spite of the name. If your business is in this league though, you will probably have many people advising you what type of system to buy; they will come up with the same answers you will be getting here. Essentially, you should buy a system without giving too much weight to the cost.

SYSTEMS FOR SMALL BUSINESS USERS

If your company is made up of one or two dozen employees, and you will be buying a system for business applications, then here are some guidelines.

The type of system you will be looking for will cost about $5,000 and will be characterized by two *disk drives*, plenty of memory storage, and lots of available *applications software*. Other factors will be a wide screen of 64 to 80 characters per line, 24 lines per screen, and an easy-to-use, well-engineered keyboard. You should have a solid, fast *line printer* that can print reports and other data rapidly.

You may choose to have someone program the system for you, but be prepared to pay tens of thousands of dollars for customized applications software.

In this type of system, available software becomes an important factor. You do not want to learn how to program the system yourself to write the applications for your business. This is possible but will take the average person hundreds or even a thousand hours to learn how to program efficiently.

Customized programs can be written by programmers that are familiar with your system. Typical programs, such as inventory, accounts receivable, and billing will take hundreds of hours, however, and you will have to pay a programmer anywhere from $10 per hour up, making your investment in customized software at least thousands of dollars. See Section II for some considerations about software.

Since you will be running your computer regularly for various types of reports and day-to-day business use, you will want a fast, high-capacity system.

You may want to consider a 16-bit computer, as described in the next chapter. These systems are more expensive, but run at two or three times the speed of older systems.

Also important in this type of operation is memory storage capacity and disk storage capacity. Memory storage refers to the amount of available user memory in which your programs are stored. Almost all systems provide enough memory to run business applications programs; typical storage is 65,536 bytes. A byte holds about one printable character. The "16-bitters" and some older systems give you more add-on memory storage (about four times as much), which provides some improvement in overall system operation.

Disk storage is important in this application, and you should aim for a system with at least two disk drives. Two disk drives make it more convenient to do maintenance operations, such as backing up the days' transactions. You have the choice of three types of disk drives—a hard disk, which stores 10 million bytes of data or more, 8-inch drives, which store ½ million or more bytes on removable *floppy diskettes,* or 5¼-inch drives, which store 160,000 or more bytes on smaller *floppy diskettes.* In general, the more capacity, the better, although the 8-inch drives are a good compromise.

You will also want a system with a video display that can display at least 64 characters per line and 16 or more lines per screen, as shown in Fig. 1-1. Many less expensive systems only display 40 characters or less per line, and this is really not enough for many applications, such as word processing. You probably would not be interested in a color display with this type of a system, although some systems give you this option.

The keyboard on the system should be a full-sized, "human-engineered" keyboard that is easy for your employees to use.

Plan on a substantial *line printer* along with your system (see Chapter 4). Units that cost from about $750 to $1,500 should give you fast printing speeds and special features.

Typical systems to look at for this type of application are the Apple® III, Radio Shack Model II or Model 16, IBM Personal Computer, Victor 9000 and many others.

SYSTEMS FOR SMALLER BUSINESSES

If you have a smaller company but still want a system for business applications, then here are some recommendations.

The type of system you will be looking for will cost about $3,500 to $5,000 and will be characterized by two *disk drives,* good memory storage, and lots of available *applications software.*

Other factors will be a wide screen of 64 to 80 characters per line, 24 lines per screen, and an easy-to-use, well-engineered keyboard.

You should have a good *line printer* that can print computer reports, but you may be able to get by with a less expensive version than a larger business, sacrificing speed of printing for cost.

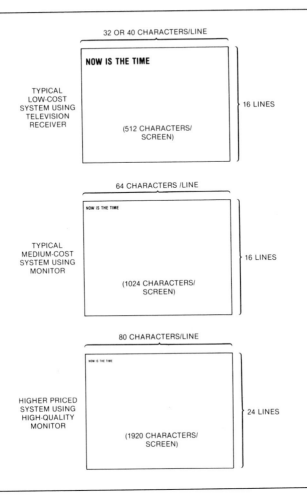

Fig. 1-1. Video display characteristics.

You may not be able to afford to have someone program the system for you, as customized software may run thousands of dollars. In this type of system, as in the previous system, available software is an important factor. You may have aspirations of learning how to program the system yourself, but if so, plan on doing this in *parallel* with running existing software. Unbelievable as it seems (in spite of the ads), some people will never be able to program a computer system efficiently!

Customized programs, again, *can* be written by programmers that are familiar with your system, but at a cost of thousands of dollars for typical programs such as inventory, accounts receivable, and billing. See Section II for some considerations about software.

You will be running your computer regularly for various types of reports and day-to-day business use and will want a moderately fast, high-capacity system. A *16-bit* microcomputer (see the next chapter) is a possibility, but be prepared to pay more for the increase in speed and memory capacity.

Memory storage does not have to be as great as the previous application but is still important. *Memory* storage refers to the amount of available user memory in which your programs are stored. Almost all systems provide enough memory to run business applications programs; typical storage is 65,536 bytes. A byte holds about one printable character.

Disk storage refers to the amount of data that can be stored on magnetic diskettes, called *floppy disks*, that your system will use. Disk storage is important in this application, and you should aim for a system with at least two disk drives. Two disk drives make it more convenient to do common operations. You can get by with one drive, but it is not recommended. Again, you have the choice of three types of disk drives: A *hard* disk, which stores 10 million bytes of data or more, 8-inch drives, which store ½ million or more bytes on removable floppy diskettes, or 5¼-inch drives, which store 160,000 or more bytes on smaller *floppy diskettes*. For low-volume business applications, two 5¼-inch drives should be adequate although it never hurts to have as much storage as possible. *Hard* drives are quite a bit more expensive, however, and probably are not necessary.

The video display on your system should display at least 64 characters per line and 16 or more lines per screen, as shown in Fig. 1-1. (Less expensive systems only display 40 characters or less per line, and this is really not enough for many applications, such as word processing.) You probably would not be interested in a color display with this type of a system although some systems will give you this option. The keyboard on the system should be a full-sized, "human-engineered" keyboard that is easy to use.

Typical systems to look at for this type of application are the Apple II, Radio Shack Model III, IBM Personal Computer, Osborne I and many others.

SYSTEMS FOR PROFESSIONAL USERS

In this type of application, you will be using the system yourself and the volume of processing that it has to do will probably not be as great as in the previous two applications, where several people might be entering data continually throughout the day. As a result, you might be able to get by with less memory and disk capacity.

The system you are looking for fills the general specifications of the system for the smaller business user, so read over the previous section. Although two disk drives are a convenience, you may want to get the initial system with one disk drive and add a second at a later time.

Again, if you are thinking of doing the programming yourself, it may take hundreds of hours to get to the point where you can write a program efficiently. Almost anyone can do simple things with a computer after a few hours, but it does take some time to become fluent in a computer language, as in other foreign languages.

If enough applications software is available for your system, however, you will be amazed at what a computer system can do for you. A good example is word processing. A word processing applications package will enable you to halve the time it takes to prepare proposals, contracts, or letters. Of course, there is some learning time before you can start using the system, but this is small (dozens of hours), compared to actually learning a programming language.

One option you might want to consider is a "letter-quality" printer. This is a slower-speed (30 to 45 characters per second) printer whose output looks like a high-quality electric typewriter. It is ideal for letters, reports, and proposals.

SYSTEMS FOR THE ENTREPRENEUR

Playing the market, eh? If you would like a system primarily to use as a tool for investments of various types and for use on a part-time basis, then it's possible to buy a fairly powerful system for $2,500 or less.

Your system can be any of the more popular small computer systems such as the Apple II, TRS-80 Model III, TRS-80 Color Computer, Commodore 64, Texas Instruments TI-99/4, or many others. It probably does not pay in this application to get a high-capacity disk system. You will probably get along nicely with a 5¼-inch disk drive or two. Unless you are using the system very infrequently, however, it is best to stay away from the *cassette-based* system. Cassette tape used in lieu of disk drives is a nuisance, unless you are making very limited use of your computer.

An important option you might want to consider for this application is *communications* capability. This is sometimes called an *RS-232C* option (see Chapter 13). With the addition of this option and a device called a *modem* (modulator/demodulator), you can link your computer over your standard home phone lines to communications networks such as Dow-Jones Information Services for on-line stock and business news, and with Compuserve or the Source, for access of literally hundreds of types of information including Associated Press news and electronic messages.

In this application you will definitely need a printer for *hard-copy* output. The printer, though, does not have to have the speed that a printer for a larger system would require. Excellent printers are available for around $500.

If you are doing a lot of graphing or plotting, then you might want to consider a system that provides a *graphics* capability. Graphics allows you to draw graphs and figures on the video display. *High-resolution graphics* refers to graphics that are very dense so that the figures and shapes are drawn in fine detail. If you have this type of system, then you will want a printer that also has graphics capability. Another consideration: Some systems, such as the Apple II, provide color displays. See Chapter 5 for a discussion of graphics.

HOUSEHOLD USE

Want to get a household computer? Now is a good time to do it. You can buy a small system for under $200. This price does not include a *display* however, and you will have to use a television set as the display device, or purchase an additional television receiver. More expensive systems will have their own *monitor* display built in.

Typical systems for household use will also have the capability of either cassette tape, or *read-only-memory* (ROM) *cartridges*. Programs for the system, including games, personal finance, or programmed instruction courses usually come on cassette tapes or in the ROM cartridge, which is about the size of a deck of playing cards and plugs into the slot on the system.

Are these systems toys? Far from it. The computer you are getting for hundreds of dollars is equivalent, in some cases, to computers costing hundreds of thousands of dollars 25 years ago! The potential is enormous even with these small systems.

One fact that we keep mentioning, however, is that it is not as easy to program the system as you think. If you plan on learning how to program computers with your home system, be prepared to spend hundreds of hours. It is relatively easy to get the computer to display simple messages and to compute simple formulas, such as the area of a circle, but another problem to write a program that will teach your child French. Fortunately, there is a good deal of applications software available at this point, and you will be able to get by very nicely without doing *any* programming.

When buying a system for this application, you would not need a lot of expensive options. Buy the basic system first, with simply the basic unit, a cassette tape recorder for input, and an optional small television receiver. You can add on later if you find that you need a printer and a disk drive. The basic unit is only a fraction of the cost of a full-blown system; in computers as with other purchases, the consumer pays dearly for options.

Typical systems for home use are the Apple II, Radio Shack Color Computer, Commodore VIC-20, Sinclair ZX-81, and the Atari 400 and 800. Prices will range from $100 for the Sinclair ZX-81 to $1,200 for the Apple II.

GAME COMPUTERS

The per capita expenditure for video games is hundreds of dollars. On that basis, it makes sense to buy a small computer system that can play about the same games as the arcade versions.

The advantage of buying a small computer over a system that will only play games is that the computer system can be expanded into other applications as well—you can program the small computer system to do a variety of different things although as we mentioned earlier in this chapter, this is sometimes a tedious task. Buy a household computer that fulfills the requirements in the previous section, and you will have a game computer as well.

COMPUTER SYSTEMS AS EXPENSIVE TOYS

Let us face it, everyone likes toys. Small computers are some of the most interesting toys in the world because they can be programmed to do all kinds of incredible things—computing your mortgage payments, balancing your checkbook, writing form letters, and storing recipes. If you would like to give computers a try, read through the applications above and try to determine which computer best suits your personal goals.

There are more similarities than differences between the systems, and you cannot go too far wrong in choosing any popular system.

WHAT DO YOU DO AFTER YOU PLUG IT IN?

After this brief introduction to small computer systems, let us continue in a different vein. Once you have the system how do you use it? What kinds of problems will you encounter? What types of *peripheral* devices are available, and how much do they cost? The following chapters try to answer in detail the question of "What do you do after you plug it in?"

Chapter

2

Should You Trade up to a 16-Bit Microcomputer?

"Hello! Welcome to Charlie's City of Computers . . ."

"What? You still have a TRS-80 Model I, Color Computer, Apple II or III, Osborne 1, Commodore VIC-20, Atari 800, or Heath H89? You haven't moved up to a new 16-bit machine? Tell you what I'm going to do . . .

"Here, look at this model. Sixteen big ones! More power, more speed . . ."

Just what is the difference between an 8-bit and a 16-bit microcomputer? Is the 16-bitter twice as good? When should you phase out your old machine and buy the new one? If you do not have a microcomputer, should you buy an 8-bitter or 16-bitter? Looking beyond the rapture of a new technology, what kinds of problems might there be with a 16-bitter that were not present on the 8-bitter? This chapter tries to answer some of these questions.

A FEW BITS OF HISTORICAL PERSPECTIVE

When an 8-bit microcomputer is talked about, what is really described is the *microprocessor* inside the microcomputer. The microprocessor is a semiconductor integrated circuit that is the heart of any microcomputer system. Let us look at a little historical perspective.

When computers were first designed in the 1940s, they consisted of thousands of vacuum tubes or relays, electronic devices about the size of a large flashlight battery. Early computers, such as the ENIAC that contained over 18,000 vacuum tubes, literally took up rooms. A typical device to store one binary digit, or on/off condition, called a *flip-flop* (as it flipped to on and flopped to off or was it the other way around?), was about 8 by 6 by 4 inches, or 512 cubic inches in these early machines.

After the invention of the transistor in the 1950s, many devices, including computers, became transistorized. The flip-flop circuit shrank to printed-circuit board size. A typical printed-circuit board version was about 4 by 8 by 1 inch, or about 32 cubic inches less than $1/10$ the size of its vacuum tube predecessor. The *central-processing unit* (CPU) of a computer now occupied one corner of a room instead of a whole room and was about the size of two large desks, one stacked on top of the other.

The next advance in computers came with the integrated circuit. Integrated circuits utilized the knowledge gained in transistor technology and are an offshoot of transistors, both being *semiconductor* devices that utilize material, such as silicon, that neither conducts electricity well, such as copper, nor is an insulating material, such as glass.

The first small-scale semiconductor devices in the 1960s fabricated the single-bit flip-flop into an integrated-circuit package measuring less than a cubic inch, less than $1/10$ the size of the transistorized version and less than $1/100$ the size of the vacuum tube version. The corresponding computer shrank to a single *bay*, about the size of a large filing cabinet. Certain small versions of computers, called *minicomputers*, shrank to a size not too much greater than today's microcomputers.

ENTER THE MICROCOMPUTER

The next advance in semiconductor technology in the 1970s culminated in a *microcomputer on a chip*. A semiconductor device now replaced the equivalent of thousands of transistorized or small-scale integrated circuit flip-flops and put most of the central-processing unit of a computer on a single chip of less

than a square inch. Here the reduction of the flip-flop was not
1/10, but more than a thousand times smaller, making *micro* computers a reality.

The Intel 4004 was one of the first microcomputers on a chip.
This device was a 4-*bit* device. It could add and subtract and
perform other operations on binary numbers that were 4 bits
long. Four-bit numbers can hold the decimal equivalents of 0
through 15 and are represented by the 4-bit binary (on/off, or 0/1)
values of 0000, 0001, 0010, 0011, 0100, 0101, 0110, 0111, 1000,
1001 1010, 1011, 1100, 1101, 1110, and 1111.

Saying that only 4-bit operations were possible does not mean to
say that numbers larger than 15 could not be handled. This is far
from the truth, as a 4-bit microprocessor such as the 4004 can
handle any size number by *stringing together* 4-bit chunks of
data. As a matter of fact, the 4004 could implement the most
complex Microsoft BASIC interpreter, given enough memory.

As the 4-bit numbers are strung together in *multiple-precision* to
enable the microprocessor to handle larger numbers, however,
there is a great deal of *overhead* or wasted time in software to
enable operations on other than 4-bits.

Instructions for the 4004 and data which the 4004 processed
were generally held in external (to the 4004) memory. To *access*
the memory, two sets of lines were used. One set, called the *data
bus,* consisted of 4 lines; all 4-bit segments of data were passed
to or from the microprocessor along these lines.

Another set of lines, called the *address bus,* held the location in
external memory in which the instruction or data was to be
found. There were the equivalent of 12 address lines on the 4004,
and up to 4096 separate locations could be addressed (you can
address 1024 locations with 10 lines, 2048 with 11 lines, 4096
with 12 lines, and so forth).

Now at this point, a question might come to your mind. Why
were only 4 data bus and the equivalent of 12 address bus lines
used? Why weren't 32 data bus lines and 32 address bus lines
used to make the microprocessor capable of processing 32 bits of

data and addressing 4 billion locations in memory? The main reason for not doing this was that it could not be done. The technology of the time permitted only so many equivalent transistors on the semiconductor chip, just enough to implement a 4-bit microprocessor.

Progress being what it is, though, the 4004 was soon followed by an improved version, the 4040, and two 8-bit microprocessors, the 8008 and 8080, which allowed operations such as adds and subtracts on 8 bits of data. Now each arithmetic operation and other operations worked with numbers ranging in size from 0 (00000000) through 255 (11111111).

The 8080 not only increased the size of data that could be processed, it increased the number of memory locations that could be addressed from 4,096 to 65,536. The data bus in the 8080 was now 8 lines and the address bus was 16 lines. The semiconductor chip itself was bigger, with 40 *pins* in place of 16 in the 4004. The *clock speed* was also increased by a factor of eight. (The clock speed is the speed at which internal microprocessor operations proceed, and the *execution speed* of each instruction is therefore directly related to the clock speed.)

Although the 8080 generally operated on data that was 8 bits in length, it allowed a few operations on data that was 16 bits in length so that numbers up to 65,535 could be processed. Of course, like the 4004, the 8080 could handle any number by *multiple-precision* operations.

Companies other than Intel produced competing products in the mid to late '70s. Chips such as the MOS Technology 6502 (used in the Apple II and III, Commodore machines, and Atari), the Motorola 6800, and the Zilog Z-80 (used in the Radio Shack Models I to III and the Osborne) were very similar to the 8080. They could add, subtract, and perform other operations on 8 bits of data, and occasionally 16 bits of data, and they had a 16-line address bus to allow 65,535 locations in memory to be addressed.

The instruction sets of these chips were also comparable. Typically there were hundreds of instructions that would allow such *machine-level* operations such as adding two 8-bit numbers, subtracting two 8-bit numbers, and transferring an 8-bit number. Every program was eventually handled at this *machine-language* level even though to the users it appeared that they were working in BASIC or FORTRAN.

The architecture of the microprocessors was also similar. All manufacturers used about the same ways of getting data and instructions in and out of memory, decoding the instructions, and handling internal operations in the microprocessor itself.

ENTER THE BIG GUNS

In the late 1970s distant guns were heard, and there were occasional flashes revealing developments of 16-bit microprocessors. In the early 1980s, these new microprocessors were finally released.

First of these was the Intel 8086. Soon after the 8086 was introduced, the Zilog Z8000 and Motorola 68000 appeared, among others. As expected, the 16-bitters were able to process 16 bits of data, allowing direct operations on numbers up to 65,535. More significantly, the number of address bus lines was increased so that 16-bitters can now directly address 1 or 8 or 16 *megabytes* (up to about 16 million bytes) of memory. Furthermore, the architecture of the new 16-bitters contained new schemes to overlap processing of one instruction and access from memory of the next instruction. In addition, *clock speeds* were more than twice as fast as even the upgraded 8080s, 6502s, and Z-80s.

THE ADVANTAGES AND DISADVANTAGES
OF PROCESSING 16 BITS

The most obvious advantage of the 16-bitters is the ability to directly add, subtract, and do other types of processing on 16 bits of data. See Fig. 2-1. Obviously, if one can add two 16-bit numbers, it will take only half the time of adding two 8-bit numbers. How much of an impact does this have on total program execution speed? For example, if you have a sort operation for inventory, which is pure computing without input/output operations, will the sort run twice as fast on a 16-bitter as an 8-bitter?

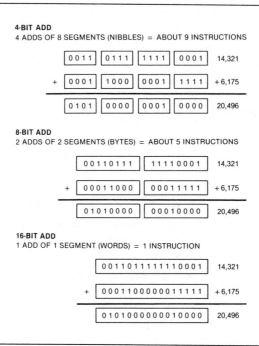

Fig. 2-1. Add operations on 4-, 8-, and 16-Bit microprocessors.

The answer is no. It is possible that in some short sets of instructions the execution speed will be more than twice as great in using a 16-bitter. However, only a small percentage of most programs actually performs arithmetic operations on data; the rest of the instructions set up *loops*, test conditions for *branching* (execution of different program paths), and do other overhead. Also, it is neither necessary nor desirable to work with larger numbers in many cases. In a loop to find the state sales tax, for example, the index of the state would be only 0 through 49, which could be held in 8 bits (or 6 bits); using 16-bit instructions might actually take longer and use a byte or so of memory more than the 8-bit operation. Another good example of this is byte-oriented data such as the *American Standard Code for Informa-*

tion Interchange (ASCII) character representation used on all current microcomputers. Again, it may actually be more efficient to bring in the characters one byte (8 bits) at a time, than to use 16-bit chunks (usually called *words*).

Of course, the optimum case is to be able to use both 8- and 16-bit data oriented instructions, and some 16-bitters will let you do just that. The point, however, is not to expect to halve the execution speed just because 16-bit operations are being done.

NEVER ENOUGH MEMORY

How desirable is it to have more memory? There is an old programmer axiom that a program always needs 1,000 bytes of memory more than you have. This was really more applicable in olden days (1965) when memory was expensive and computers had only 4,096 bytes of memory. In general, most games, programmed instruction courses, and nonbusiness programs use only a portion of the 64K bytes of memory found in current microcomputers such as the TRS-80 Model II, Apple II, and Atari 800. Most significant business, word processing, and scientific processing programs, on the other hand, could use the additional memory.

The effect of having more memory will be to reduce the number of disk operations, as more data or program segments can be kept in memory at one time. If the program performs many disk operations, this will speed up overall program "throughput." How much? Depending upon the amount of disk activity, anywhere from a negligible amount to 10% or more.

Are there any disadvantages in having more memory addressing capability? Probably not. There is the increased development cost of the chip, but this is buried in the total cost of the system.

THE EFFECT OF SPEED

It was mentioned earlier that the newer 16-bitters have increased clock speed. This will be a definite advantage, increasing the execution speed of programs in proportion to the increase in clock speed. A 16-bit computer with a clock speed that is double that of a current 8-bitter will double the program execution speed, although a direct comparison probably would not be possible because of the difference in instruction sets of the 8- and 16-bitter.

EXPANDED INSTRUCTION SETS

How about the instruction sets of the 16-bitters? Will they dramatically affect the execution speeds of programs? Many of the instructions of the new 16-bitters are very similar to the old. Marketing blurbs notwithstanding, instruction sets have changed very little over the past ten years or so, and you would not see new, powerful instructions that perform operations such as "add two numbers and branch if this is a Tuesday."

An exception to this, however, is that all of the new microprocessors will have *hardware* multiply and divides. Incredible as it seems, the microprocessors currently used in most microcomputers have no built-in multiplies and divides, and these operations must be implemented in software. See Fig. 2-2. The 16-bit microprocessor multiplies and divides speed up these operations to make them 10 or 20 times as fast or more! Again, this can have a significant impact on certain program segments, but

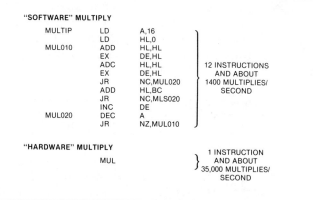

Fig. 2-2. Machine-level multiplies.

is diluted by the overhead of a large program. In certain number-crunching operations, the execution speed of a program could be increased 10 times or more; in most programs you may see a 10% increase in speed or so.

NEW DESIGNS IN ARCHITECTURE

How about the new design concepts mentioned earlier? The new design concepts are an important bonus. The 16-bitters will generally be making a memory access for the next instruction while the current instruction is being executed, on the assumption that the next instruction will follow the current. This assumption becomes invalid for branches but is true for most code. Since memory access is a major portion of instruction processing time, this overlap will increase the "throughput" by almost 33% in some cases.

SUMMING IT ALL UP . . .

What do you have when you consider the above? Multiply 2 for an increase in clock rate, 1.3 for overlapped execution and "fetch," 1.1 for fast mutiplies, 1.1 for the reduced overhead of more memory, and you get a microprocessor that is over 3 times as fast, in addition to offering more memory. How can you lose?

"So you see, my friend, there's no reason not to buy one of these new beauties from Charlie's Computers. Think of yourself, tooling along, sorting your accounts receivables at three times the speed . . ."

Ah, but you can lose. . . . Here's how.

LOSING THE 16-BIT GAME

It is not obvious yet that 16-bitters have made it. Oh certainly, ten years from now, most microcomputers will be 16-bitters or more. However, if you buy a 16-bitter too soon you will have these problems:

- Much software development in BASIC, other languages, operating systems, and from software manufacturers remains to be done in some cases. Software development takes an enormous amount of time and money, and some companies have not made the commitment because they do not know if 16-bitters will sell well. And you have not bought a 16-bitter because you do not know whether they will be popular. . . .

- You will be faced with lack of application software. The 8080, 6800, 6502, and Z-80 have been around for a long time and there is a tremendous amount of software available for these microprocessors in general and for microcomputers built around them. Existing software helps in development of other applications software. Software for the new machines will not, in general, be able to utilize old software, and it will take several years to develop the new software to the degree it exists on current systems.

If the 16-bit machines do not catch on, you will have neither the quantity of development software (operating systems and the like) nor the quantity of applications software (much of it generated by cottage industry when there is a large enough user base to make it profitable).

CIRCULAR REASONING HERE?

If all of this sounds like circular reasoning, it is. The 16-bitters are attractive but not an order of magnitude better than the existing machines. Microcomputer users are not rushing to replace their existing systems with 16-bit versions. Because there is not the overwhelming interest, many manufacturers have not made the commitment. The situation could change at any minute with an announcement of a dramatic new model from Apple Computer, Inc., Tandy Corp., or IBM, Inc. For now, though, the situation is somewhat static.

CURRENT 16-BITTERS

There are a number of current microcomputers that fit into the 16-bit category. The IBM Personal Computer uses an 8088, which is based upon the Intel 8086, but is not as powerful. It is somewhat an 8-bit version of a 16-bit microprocessor. Response to the

IBM PC has been excellent, and this may speed acceptance of the 16-bitters in general.

The Radio Shack Model 16 uses a Motorola 68000 in a plug-in board on their Model II computer. In this case, the 68000 board makes the 16 a true 16-bitter. This concept, by the way, of new, more powerful microprocessors on replacement plug-in modules is perfectly valid and may also hasten acceptance of 16-bitters for S-100 type computers (or CP/M type) machines, as a number of manufacturers make 16-bit microprocessor boards for S-100 systems.

A number of companies that are not necessarily small companies, but have less penetration into the small computer marketplace, have current 16-bit microcomputers—companies such as Altos, Corvus, and Fortune Systems. Models of 16-bit microcomputers by such companies as Apple Computer, Inc., Tandy Corp., and others have not been formally announced at this time but are rumored to be under development. Maybe you have discarded your 8-bitter for a 16-bitter long ago. On the other hand, you may still be waiting for that other guy to create the enthusiasm you did not have . . .

"Now about that trade-in . . . I had the computer maintenance man check it out. He found that pressure was down in the CPU section and that somebody had set back the clock . . . Afraid we can't give you what we were talking about. But you're going to love this '16-banger' . . ."

Chapter

3

Storage for the Masses — RAM Storage and Disk Drives

When the MITS Altair 8800 computer, the first personal computer, was introduced in 1976, it offered 1024 bytes of RAM (random-access memory) storage! Today we talk in terms of hundreds of thousands of bytes of storage for RAM and millions of bytes of storage for disk drives.

How much storage is necessary? Surely thousands of bytes in RAM is enough, and certainly millions of bytes on disk would be overkill! Depending upon the application, however, it is relatively easy to use up hundreds of thousands of bytes. If you have an inventory of 5,000 items, for example, and each item has a 100-byte record describing it (part number, description, number on hand, number on order, and so forth), you have used up ½ million bytes. Another example: If you belong to CompuServe or The Source and have access to on-line communications data, it would take only about 4½ hours to fill up ½ million bytes of storage in memory or on disk at 30 characters per second.

Remember the axiom of the programmer from the previous chapter: Programs always require more memory than the space available!

Although this is becoming less valid in these days of inexpensive memory, it does point out that programs have a tendency to expand to fill all the RAM space available.

This chapter looks at the forms of *mass storage*, paying particular attention to RAM and disk storage. Roughly, mass storage can be divided into semiconductor memory, magnetic tape, and magnetic disk.

SEMICONDUCTOR MEMORY

The Apple II, TRS-80 Model III, and a lot of other small computers are limited to 64K (65,536) bytes of memory. As a result, a lot of the available software will only work in that limited addressing range. For some programs that does not matter, but if the user memory is there, other programs will take advantage of it, without having to do time-consuming disk operations.

The memory price is not as expensive as you might think. Right now you can get 64K of user RAM (random-access memory) for about $540. Putting it another way, that is about 0.8 cent per byte.

Just as a point of reference, that 0.8 cent per byte is about the same for other plug-in memory boards. A 64K byte memory board for CP/M type systems would be about the same price.

Some computers have empty memory sockets, though, and adding memory is as easy as plugging in a few chips. That's true on the IBM Personal Computer up to 64K, for example, and on other systems. If you add memory this way, the price of additional memory is less expensive—about $50 per 16K, or about 0.3 cent per byte.

Actually, the IBM PC is not the only small computer that will let you get lots of user RAM. There are other ones that allow you to add *memory banking*.

No, this has nothing to do with T-Bill accounts . . . In this type of banking you can add additional RAM even though the basic architecture was not designed for it. Take the Apple III. It is basically built around a 6502 microprocessor, which has a 64K addressing range. You can add additional 32K byte banks up to 256K. These banks can be selected by the operating system, and you are not even aware that they are there.

User RAM, by the way, is fast. Any additional RAM you add can be accessed at the same speed as basic RAM. And that is about one byte every 5 microseconds or less.

MAGNETIC TAPE

The next option for mass storage is *magnetic tape*. Magnetic tape was used a lot on larger computer systems. These systems had 7- and 9-track mag tapes (that is 7 or 9 heads across the width of the tape!) as stock storage devices, typically bay after bay of them. Tape was (and is) an inexpensive way to store data. A total of 25 million bytes can be stored on a 2,400-foot reel. That puts the cost at about $1/5{,}000$ less expensive than RAM memory storage.

Data access on tape, though, is very slow. Tape data has to be accessed sequentially. You have to start the tape at the beginning, and then read through one record of data at a time until you find what you are looking for.

If the data is at the end of the tape, it might take ten minutes to find the data required, and that is for the case of a large computer system.

Cassette tapes on small computers do not work much differently. If anything, they are less efficient.

Most small computers read cassette data at rates of about 25 to 120 bytes per second. Assume that a C90 cassette tape is being used. A time of 45 minutes on one side of a C90 cassette is 2,700 seconds. At a data rate of 120 bytes per second, that represents storage of about 324,000 bytes. Unfortunately, data cannot be packed into the tape continuously. You have to leave *inter-record* gaps every few hundred bytes or so; so a good practical approximation to the storage on cassette tape would be about 162,000 bytes on one side of a C90 cassette.

The same problem exists in locating a particular piece of data, however, as on the larger tape machines. The worst-case condition would occur when the data you were looking for was at the end of the tape, and that would be about 45 minutes! Of course, you could cheat a little by looking at the counter on the recorder and doing a fast forward manually.

Magnetic tape on small computers, though, is cheap storage— about 0.002 cent per byte.

DISK DRIVE STORAGE

Disk drives come in two sizes, 8 inch and 5¼ inch. The sizes refer to the size of the *diskette* that is put into the drive. Each 5¼ inch diskette looks somewhat like a 45-RPM recording of "Rock Around the Clock"; the 8 inch is a somewhat larger version.

Each diskette has recorded data not in grooves but on a magnetic path in similar fashion to audio tape, Every disk drive has a read/write *head*, similar to the audio tape recorder head, that writes and reads a magnetic pattern from the disk.

Unlike a 45-RPM record, data is not recorded in a spiral fashion into the center of the disk. It is recorded on *tracks* which are concentric circles as shown in Fig. 3-1. The disk drive can position the head over any track by stepping in or out one track at a time until it finds the right track.

Once the disk drive has been told (by the computer program) to find the proper track, it does so, and then reports back to the program that it is now positioned over the track. The number of tracks depends upon the disk drive used with your system— there may be 35, 40, 77, or other numbers of tracks.

Not only can data be located by track, it can be located by *sector*. A sector is a subdivision of a track, as shown in Fig. 3-2. The number of sectors also depends upon the type of disk drive used in your computer system and may vary from 10 to 18 or more.

The diskette in a disk drive is spinning at about 300 revolutions per minute, more than six times as fast as the 45-RPM record. It takes no longer than ¹/₅ of a second for any sector to spin around under the head once the proper track has been found.

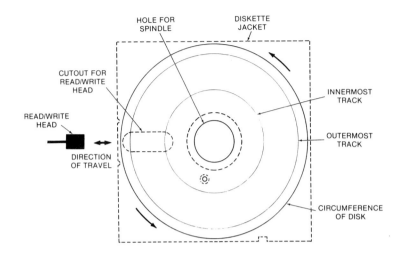

Fig. 3-1. Diskette tracks.

The amount of data that can be held on a single diskette again varies with the system. Generally, 256 bytes of data can be held per sector. The total number of bytes that can be held on a single side of a diskette is 256 times the number of sectors per track times the number of tracks per diskette.

The original 8-inch disk drive could hold about 250,000 bytes and had removable 8-inch diskettes. Not too long after the 8-inch disk drive was introduced, the 5¼-inch drive came out. It could hold about 90,000 bytes at first.

Later both the 8-inch and 5¼-inch drives were redesigned to *double density,* making the diskette capacity about 500,000 bytes and 160,000 bytes, respectively. A little later, *quad density* drives were introduced, making the capacity about a million bytes and 320,000 bytes.

The magnetic diskette manufacturers maintain that they are ready for the disk drive *hardware* to go to even greater capacities per diskette, so the limit on disk storage density has not been reached yet.

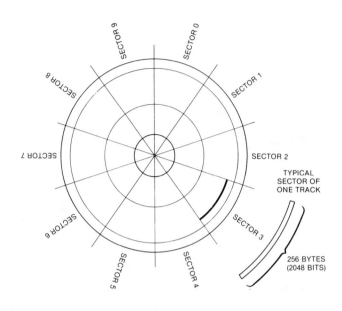

Fig. 3-2. Diskette sectors.

A new development is the 3-inch drive used in the Sinclair Spectrum computer. It has about a 100,000-byte capacity. There are some other manufacturers coming out with 3-inch drives, also.

Another recent development is *hard drives,* most of which are the so-called "winchester" drives.

The hard drives do not have a removable diskette. They have a permanent hard-surfaced disk with a *floating head.* If you look at the cost of storage on the 5¼ inch, 8 inch, and hard drives, you will find something like:

    5¼ inch: 0.0025 cent per byte
    8 inch: 0.0014 cent per byte
    Hard drives: 0.035 cent per byte

The hard drives are fairly reliable. I won't say that they *never* crash, but the disk is sealed and free from contamination that might cause disk wear and tear. It is best to back them up by duplicating files on other disk drives with removable diskettes, though.

Should you buy a hard disk? It depends upon your application. If you are doing *storage intensive* processing with a lot of data, it may be practical to get a hard disk drive.

Also, the hard disk is fairly reliable. There should not be any disk malfunctions. That means the data is there when you want it, and you would not have to go searching through sixty 5¼-inch diskettes to find a certain file.

It is truly amazing how many diskettes full of programs and data you can collect over a year or so. There are a lot of small computer users who have far more than the 60 diskettes that would fill up a 10 megabyte Winchester drive.

CASSETTES VERSUS DISKS

If you are currently using a cassette with your computer, you know that programs and other data are read *sequentially* from the cassette tape. You have to start the tape at the beginning, wait until the computer finds the proper *file*, and then wait until the computer reads in the program or data. With a C90 sized cassette, this can be rather time consuming—in some cases, it may take longer than it takes to read this chapter!

With a disk drive, however, data can be read or written at random. Well, not really at random—that would be chaos! *Random access* really means that any track and sector can be found by the disk drive in less than one second by positioning the head over the track and waiting until the proper sector spins around under the head.

What all of the above discussion means is that the disk drive offers a means to store large amounts of data and to access that data in seconds rather than minutes. Furthermore, no operator intervention is needed. You do not have to position a cassette tape to the proper point, and then switch to another cassette for the next program. Disk drives in a system give the computer system a chance to do things automatically—to speed up the overall efficiency of the system.

BUBBLE MEMORIES AND OTHER DEVICES

Bubble memories were highly touted as disk replacements for several years. They are being used in some peripherals and by the military, but we probably will not see them in widespread use in small computers. They rely on magnetic bubbles and require about half the *support logic* of disk drives.

Another interesting new item is a RAM that looks like a disk! The RAM plugs in as a memory board but is addressed as disk. The system still goes ahead and makes disk input/output calls, but the RAM is accessed in lieu of the disk. In this design the RAM emulates a disk drive. One of the problems, however, is that you need a computer with a large enough memory addressing range to use it. Microsoft is one manufacturer who markets such a device, which is the RAMCard for the IBM PC.

The advantage is that the RAM *pseudo-disk* operates at 50 times the speed of the actual disk. The disadvantage is that the data is volatile. It disappears as soon as you turn the power off.

And that brings up another interesting point. The trend now is towards low-power memories. Most ordinary RAM memory loses the data as soon as the system is switched off. Some of the pocket computers, however, retain the contents of memory by supplying power when the computer is not being used. That is possible if low-power memory like CMOS (Complementary Metal Oxide Semiconductor) memory is used. We may see the larger computers using the same type of nonvolatile memory.

In spite of all of the new developments, it appears we are going to see current RAM memory types and disks being the dominant memories in the next few years. RAM is getting less expensive, and we will see a lot larger user memory because of the greater memory capability of the 16-bit computers like your IBM PC. We are also going to see much less expensive hard disks and floppy disks—probably half of what the costs are now—in several years.

46

CHECK LIST FOR MASS STORAGE DEVICES

RAM

- Can you add the RAM chips yourself? Even though the manufacturers would not advertise the fact, you may be able to partially upgrade your system by simply plugging in commonly available RAM chips at a fraction of the cost for what they would charge. Check your local user group to see if this is feasible.
- If you must add RAM memory boards, check alternate suppliers. Most small computer companies have secondary manufacturers for the memory devices, and their prices are competitive.
- Of course, there is the old "void-your-warranty" problem for adding memory other than RAM chips from the manufacturer or memory plug-in boards. If a failure occurs in the RAM or the plug-in board, you may not be able to get service from the manufacturer.
- If you upgrade to more RAM, will your existing applications software be able to take advantage of it? Some programs do not need the additional memory; others need it but will not be able to take advantage of it. This is most true on systems with a larger addressing range, such as the 16-bit machines.

Cassette Tape

- Do you require a lot of mass storage? If so, consider buying a disk system. There is a high initial investment, but you soon earn it back with your time saved. Cassette tape is not a good mass storage medium (remember the Cruncher).
- If you do not require a great deal of mass storage but simply want to load programs quickly, consider a device like the Exatron Stringy Floppy™. This is a high-speed cassette tape geared to rapid load programs and data but not to large amounts of data storage.

Soft Disks

- Do you need a greater capacity for your disk? Unless you have a 320K, 5¼-inch drive, or a 500K, 8-inch drive, the answer is usually yes. It does not take long to fill up 160K worth of diskette space.
- Use the greatest density for your system available. Some manufacturers offer upgrades to a larger capacity disk (Radio Shack for their Model I, IBM for their PC). Other manufacturers offer 8-inch disk drives or *double-density* drives to upgrade your current system.
- Should you get multiple drives? In most cases the software from the computer manufacturer will not span from one drive to the next. In other words, you cannot continue a file from one drive to the next. The primary advantage more drives will give you, then, is the convenience of not having to insert a new diskette. On the other hand, two drives are a decided advantage to one drive for such things as doing *backups* and copying files. Two drives are practical, but more than two drives may not be.
- Should you buy cheap diskettes? No, not unless you like losing data. How important is your time in reconstructing the programs and data on the diskettes?

Hard Drives

The old familiar problems come up with an expensive piece of equipment like a hard drive:

- First, do you really need that much storage? Extrapolate your mass storage usage by finding out at what rate you use up diskettes. For example, if you use four 160K diskettes a month, then you have enough space on a 10-megabyte hard drive for about 15 months worth of data.
- Does your computer manufacturer offer a hard drive? If so, it may be best to buy one from the manufacturer, avoiding these problems:

    1. When the drive malfunctions, you will be able to have it repaired by the computer system manufacturer. This avoids "finger-pointing" about which part of the system is actually at fault.

2. The operating system software may not be equipped to support a *foreign* hard drive. There are exceptions to this, a notable example being LDOS for the TRS-80s that will support many different drive configurations.

- If your computer system manufacturer does not offer a hard drive, and you would like one, then use this check list:

  1. Will the hard drive run with existing operating system software, or will a new operating system or *patches* be necessary? Do the patches work?!
  2. What kind of warranty is provided? Six months to one year is reasonable.
  3. Is local repair offered? If not, what is the turnaround time for getting the system repaired?
  4. Times are tough. Will the company be around a year from now to service the unit?

- What kind of backup will you use on the hard drive? Plan on doing systematic backups and maintaining a configuration log of what files you have on the drive. Backing up 10 megabytes of hard disk requires 62, 160K mini-floppies! Special magnetic tape backup may be available, but at a high price.

Line Printers — A Way To Get Hard Copy

Buying a small computer system, as you've probably discovered, is unlike many other major purchases. If you buy a car, you can add a few options such as whitewalls or stereo radio for a fraction of the basic price, If you buy a new house, the builder will offer such niceties as carpeting or a trash compactor for a nominal cost. However, the neophyte, small-computer system buyer soon finds that the cost of the microcomputer itself is perhaps only 30% to 40% of the total cost of the computer system. The remainder of the cost is the price of disk drives, line printers, and other peripherals. No wonder so many hospital trauma centers have been added nationwide since the advent of the small computer!

Line printers generally cost more than any other computer system component, and for that reason, it pays to spend some time in considering options. In this chapter, you will get some background on the types of line printers that are available and tips on avoiding common problems associated with line printers.

TYPES OF LINE PRINTERS

Line printers for small computers can be put into several different categories, as shown in Fig. 4-1:
1. Dot-matrix printers
2. Dot-matrix printers with graphics
3. Character printers

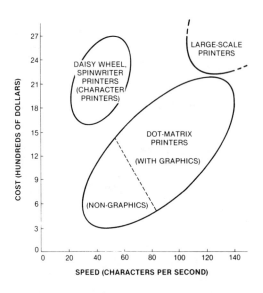

COST (HUNDREDS OF DOLLARS)

DAISY WHEEL,
SPINWRITER
PRINTERS
(CHARACTER
PRINTERS)

LARGE-SCALE
PRINTERS

DOT-MATRIX
PRINTERS

(WITH GRAPHICS)

(NON-GRAPHICS)

SPEED (CHARACTERS PER SECOND)

Fig. 4-1. Small-computer printers.

These categories are roughly grouped in order of price. Prices range from about $400 to over $2,000.

Let us first discuss these general types in detail and then look at some of the other aspects of choosing a printer for your system.

DOT-MATRIX PRINTERS

Dot-matrix printers have been around for some time, even before the advent of personal computers. A character is printed by combining rows of dots, similar to the usual video display of character data. See Fig. 4-2. Because the character is small, the eye integrates the dots into a single character. The dot matrix is usually a 5-by-7 dot-matrix although the trend is to use a larger matrix, such as 9 by 9.

Dot-matrix printers are usually much less expensive to manufacture than other types of printers. Prices range from about $400 up to $2,000.

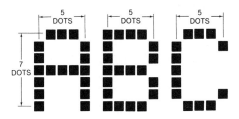

Fig. 4-2. Dot-matrix printing.

DOT-MATRIX PRINTERS WITH GRAPHICS

Earlier types of dot-matrix printers (three years or so ago) were capable of printing common characters, usually the characters A through Z in upper and lower case, the digits 0 through 9, and a set of special characters such as the pound or number (#) or the percent (%)—in general about the same characters you see on a microcomputer (or typewriter) keyboard. In some cases, the number of characters per line could be changed, or an expanded character size could be printed.

In the past few years, however, "creeping elegance" has set in. Dot-matrix printers are getting smarter and smarter. The reason for this is that the "innards" of the electronic components of line printers are being replaced with microprocessor chips. Instead of printing one set of typewriterlike characters, virtually any symbol that can be defined by a matrix of dots can be printed.

Expanded Character Sets

Previous line printers had to use *discrete logic*—individual electronic components—to print characters. It was difficult to translate the codes for various characters into a dot-matrix print action in a few parts at low cost. With microprocessors, however, all of the translation is done in *firmware*, hardwired software in read-only memory (ROM). This has resulted in printing of virtually any character, including foreign language characters such as tildes (˜ and umlauts (¨), or Latin, Greek, and Kata-Kana symbols. Even user-defined symbols can be printed in some print-ers—the codes defining the characters are output to the line printer by a BASIC (or other) program.

Intelligent Printing

Another feature found in the newer printers is *intelligent print-ing.* The most common type of intelligent printing is *bidirec-tional printing.*

In older printers each character was printed as soon as it was received. In the new dot-matrix printers, the microprocessor looks at each character as it comes in, stores it in a buffer, and then makes decisions about how to print it most efficiently.

Let us look at an example of this. Suppose we wanted to print the text shown in Fig. 4-3. The text is centered in the middle of the page. In an old-style printer (going back five years or so), the text would be printed as 200 characters plus four *line feeds.* The line feed is similar to the typewriter carriage return. If the printer printed each character in $1/25$ of a second and took $1/4$ of a second to carriage return from the 50 print position, it would take about nine seconds to print the text. Most of the time would be spent in spacing over to the column (printing blank characters) and in performing carriage returns.

In a new-style dot-matrix printer, however, the microprocessor would assemble all of the 204 characters in a buffer and then print them as shown in Fig. 4-4, using both forward and reverse printing. Neat, eh? Because only 40 spaces plus 24 characters (all nonblank) were printed, and no carriage returns were done, the print time would be under three seconds, more than three times as fast as the old-style printer!

Graphics Printing

Another feature found in the new dot-matrix printers is graphics printing. Most microcomputers have some graphics capabilities, and some, such as the Apple computer, have excellent high-resolution graphics. Up to a few years ago, there was no means to get a *hard copy* of the graphics, at least at a reasonable price. (Large-scale systems use plotters that cost $10,000 or more.)

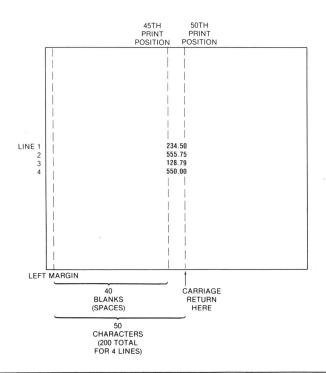

Fig. 4-3. Print example.

Newer printers will print excellent high-resolution graphics, though, and at great prices. One example that comes to mind is the Radio Shack Line Printer VII, a dot-matrix printer that sells for under $400 and will print character data or graphics data of 60 dots per inch horizontally by 63 dots vertically.

Dot-matrix printers that offer graphics capability can reproduce screen graphics in full detail, albeit black and white.

Variable Pitch, Line and Character Spacing

Another option offered by the newer dot-matrix printers is that of being able to alter character size, line spacing, and character spacing.

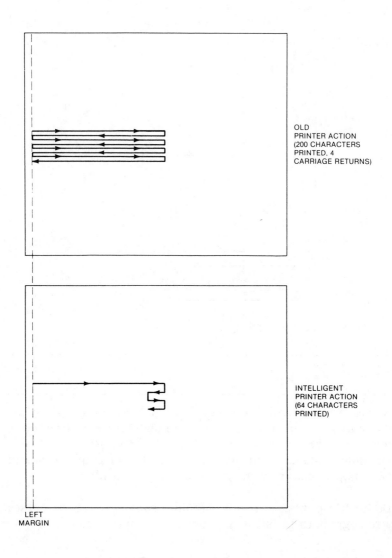

OLD
PRINTER ACTION
(200 CHARACTERS
PRINTED. 4
CARRIAGE RETURNS)

INTELLIGENT
PRINTER ACTION
(64 CHARACTERS
PRINTED)

LEFT
MARGIN

Fig. 4-4. Intelligent printing.

The normal character size is 10 characters per inch. This permits about 80 characters on an 8½-inch form, with left and right margins. Many dot matrix printers now allow you to alter the pitch under program control. The Heath/Zenith 25 Printer, for example, provides 10, 12, 13.2, and 16.5 characters per inch, all under software control.

Normal vertical line spacing is 6 lines per inch. This is usually less flexible than character spacing and a typical printer may allow either 6 or 8 lines per inch.

Some dot-matrix printers offer *proportional spacing*. This mode uses variable spacing between characters based on the width of each character, as in typesetting. The result is hard copy that looks very pleasing to the eye, an important factor for business correspondence and other applications.

Ink Versus Electrical Printing

A word should be said here about dot-matrix print methods. Most of the newer dot-matrix printers print ink by impact. Some types, however, print *burn spots* by passing an electrical current through the print head and by using a special electro-sensitive paper. My personal preference would be to avoid the printers that use electro-sensitive (aluminized) paper, simply because of the inconvenience in paper supplies and higher cost. The quality in some cases is excellent, however.

CHARACTER PRINTERS

The third major group of small computer system printers is the *character-printer* group. These are printers primarily designed to produce high-quality copy, almost equal to typeset copy in some cases. Character printers generally run from $1,600 to $2,500 or more.

Character printers are *impact-type* printers, The character is printed by striking a hammer against a metal or plastic casting of the character,

The two most popular printers in this group are the *daisy-wheel* and *spinwriter* character printers.

Daisy-wheel printers, such as Diablo (Xerox, Inc.) and other manufacturers, use a metal or plastic daisy wheel that looks like a daisy or sunburst. The wheel is rotated to the proper position. The NEC Spinwriter uses a similar concept except that a thimble is rotated in place of the daisy wheel.

The daisy wheel and spinwriter character printers print on the order of 30 to 60 characters per second, depending upon the manufacturer. This may be up to five times or so slower than a dot-matrix printer.

The advantage of the daisy wheel and spinwriter is that the character sets and type fonts may be easily changed by switching the daisy wheel or thimble. A large variety of character sets are offered. Proportional spacing is also provided, under proper program control.

Graphics is also possible on these printers, usually at 120 dots per inch horizontally by 48 dots vertically. The graphics must be under program control and is accomplished by printing a period or other character for each dot, a laborious task compared to the dot-matrix graphics capabilities.

PRINTER PITFALLS

Now for some of the principal problems of printers (sorry). Most of these are not from printer design or operation, but derive from trying to interface the printer from one manufacturer to a microcomputer of another manufacturer. Chief among these is the serial/parallel problem.

Serial Versus Parallel

Some printers come in a *serial form* or *parallel form*. Others come in both forms, switch selectable. The trend is to offer both versions in the same package.

Serial printers interface to the computer system via the system serial, or RS-232C, port. Parallel printers interface to a special parallel port implemented by a special board option or standard system option.

One friend received an NEC Spinwriter in serial configuration as a gift. It is an excellent printer and he loves the print quality. In the past year, however, he has spent about 100 hours converting programs so that he can use the spinwriter on his TRS-80 Model III. He would have been much better off getting the parallel version of the NEC Spinwriter. On the other hand, some systems are a perfect match for serial printers, such as CP/M-based systems, which are structured in software for serial devices.

In general, if your computer system accepts both, buy a parallel printer over the serial printer. There are two reasons for this.

First, serial printers act similarly to data communications devices such as *modems* or data terminals. They receive data strung out as a series of bits over a single pair of wires, rather than 8 bits at a time. Because of this, it may not be possible to run the printer at its maximum speed, or it may take special modifications to the line printer cable.

Secondly, the serial printer may require special software drivers. Standard software for BASIC program listing or printing may be set up for the system line printer, a parallel device. You may have to insert a serial software driver to replace the standard system software to operate the serial printer. Although that replacement may not be difficult for an experienced programmer, you may have to do the insertion for each separate applications program you use.

Label Pasting

Most microcomputer manufacturers do not manufacture their own printers. Many are adept at taking a model from a printer manufacturer and pasting their own label on the printer.

It may be possible to get the same printer from a computer store at a much lower price than from the microcomputer manufacturer. Typically the price will be several hundred dollars less per thousand dollars. If you do this, make certain that you are getting the same model.

You may have to buy a cable for the printer to fit your microcomputer. In some cases, cables are not available separately, and you will have to have one specially made. Many computer stores can do this but will probably charge at least $50 for the work.

The biggest risk in buying an equivalent printer is that the manufacturer of your microcomputer may offer a better warranty for the printer and quicker and less expensive repair than the printer manufacturer. Expect the printer to fail once per year and investigate the repair action you are going to take and the availability of repair services.

Special Software

In addition to special software for serial printers, you may require special software drivers to make full use of the options on your printer.

This is a common scenario in computer stores:

CUSTOMER: Does this printer give you true proportional spacing?

CLERK: Yes, look at the manual—proportional spacing!

CUSTOMER: Oh yeah. Will it run on my computer system?

CLERK: Well, it's all under program control. . . . Simply a matter of software . . .

The "simply a matter of software" is one of the most frightening phrases in the small computer area. In fact, writing a software driver for proportional spacing is not easy! (I've done it!) Using other printer options may require anything from changing switch settings in your computer system to hundreds of hours of programming time. Be wary!

TRACTOR FEED VERSUS FRICTION FEED

Some printers offer a choice of traction feed versus friction feed. Which is better? If you are printing an occasional letter, then friction feed may be the best choice. Friction feed allows you to use regular paper, inserted between the rollers as you require. In general, though, tractor feed is the better choice, Some printers offer only tractor feed.

Tractor feed uses special line-printer paper that has feed holes on either side. After printing, the left and right margins are torn off, and the result is usually 8½ inches wide. The paper is as inexpensive as friction feed paper—about $40 for a box of 3,000 sheets.

The chief advantage of tractor feed is that the feed is exact—each page can be positioned at exactly the right line over many pages of printing; this facilitates report or form printing where the position of the printing is fixed.

PRINTING WIDTH

I'll admit it. I'm an 8½ inch bigot. Even when I programmed in industry, I'd tear down the 14⅞-inch paper listings to 8½ inches to fit in notebooks. Some printers will accept only 8½-inch wide paper, while other printers will print up to 13.5 inches horizontally per line. Much of the computing industry uses the wider paper for reports, but the paper is unwieldy and requires special notebooks and filing cabinets.

Your BASIC interpreter and system software may not handle more than 80 characters per line for line printers, so verify this before choosing a line printer that will handle wider paper.

TIED UP IN RIBBONS AND HEADS

I have two line printers at present. One uses standard ribbons that cost about $5 each and that last for a very long time. The other requires special ribbons that I can buy only from the microcomputer manufacturer. They last for a very short time, they are never in stock, and I pay a premium price. (About $13 each for only several weeks of printing.) If you do a lot of printing, this is a serious consideration.

Another factor about line-printer ribbons—if you are interested in high-quality printing and would like to use *carbon* ribbons, make certain that these are obtainable for the line printer you are considering. Many line printers will only use *fabric-type* ribbons.

Another replacement item that the buyer usually does not think of is print heads. Dot-matrix printers require a new print head every thousand hours or so. Check how much these print heads cost and how difficult they are to get. Some printers have heads that can be replaced by the user; others require jet-engine repair experience.

TO SUM IT ALL UP

As in other microcomputer products, you are choosing a line printer at a good time. Line printers are much less expensive and offer a great deal more capability now than ever before. Consider the pitfalls described earlier when buying, and you may avoid at least some of the trauma associated with financing additional equipment for your computer system. After you have bought your line printer perhaps we can talk about some of the other equipment you should add—from this point on the whitewalls are less expensive!

Chapter

5

What Do People See in High-Resolution Graphics?

One of the large-scale computer systems in which I was involved acquired data from a jumbo jet in flight. Such things as speed, pressure, and stresses on aircraft surfaces were displayed on a large, high-resolution, color display. We were behind in programming but had to show the executives from the aircraft company *something!* The programmers were nonplussed . . .

"Let's just display the 'graph skeletons' without any actual graphics data," said one of our junior programmers. And that is what we did. Two vice-presidents stood entranced in front of a multimillion dollar data acquisition system watching graphs with headings and axes, but without any actual data. They were ecstatic!

Does this have any parallel in small computing systems? In this chapter we will explore some of the pitfalls in being "entranced by graphics." In doing so you will get a short tutorial on graphics, from "low-res" to "high-res," and from black and white to dazzling color.

A TYPICAL DISPLAY

A display is worth a thousand bytes, so we have created a representative display in Fig. 5-1.

The smallest unit that can be turned "on" or "off" on the display is a *picture element, pixel* for short. The resolution of both

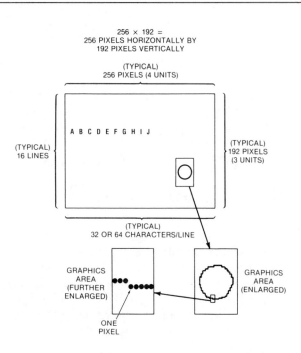

Fig. 5-1. Typical graphics display.

high-resolution graphics and low-resolution graphics is expressed in terms of pixels. The normal meaning of a 640-by-200 display is 640 pixels horizontally by 200 pixels vertically. The total number of pixels on a screen full of graphics is the horizontal number times the vertical number; in the case of the 640-by-200 display, a screen full of graphics data would be made up of 128,000 pixels!

You may wonder why the number of horizontal pixels is usually greater than the number of vertical pixels. This is because each pixel is evenly spaced and the standard television picture is of uniform aspect ratio. The aspect ratio is the width compared to the height, which is normally 4:3. A resolution of 256 by 192 (as, for example, the Texas Instruments TI-99/4) works out to exactly 4:3 (256:192). Other systems compromise on this aspect ratio based on memory storage and electronics design (the Commodore PET is 320 by 200, for example, or 4.8:3).

One of the most common things to be displayed on any personal computer system is alphanumeric characters. Alphanumeric displays were common long before graphics displays. Every microcomputer has the capability of displaying alphanumeric data. This is almost always done by means of a *character-generator*, embedded within the control logic of the microcomputer. The character generator defines a character by using a 5-by-7 matrix of pixels, or, in other cases, a larger matrix. Fig. 5-2 shows several characters made up of a matrix of 5 by 7 pixels.

Because a *block* of pixels is used for one character, the display of alphanumeric data is usually divided up into *lines* and *character positions* along the line. The number of lines and character positions is related to the resolution of the display—the number of pixels that can be displayed horizontally and vertically.

The concept of a block may also be carried through in graphics modes. Although the highest resolution graphics mode might result in defining one pixel worth of display, lower resolution modes will group pixels into blocks of elements.

MONITORS AND MODULATORS

There are basically two types of displays provided on today's high-resolution color computers. Some microcomputers, such as the Color Computer from Radio Shack, are meant to be used exclusively with a standard television receiver. Other microcomputers, such as the IBM Personal Computer with color graphics option, and the Apple II, provide an output that can be plugged into a *monitor*, a higher quality display. However, the latter type can also be used with an inexpensive *modulator* to provide display on a standard television receiver.

Why the difference? The difference is that standard black and white or color television receivers operate with less resolution than the more expensive monitor. About the maximum resolution that can be obtained with a television receiver is 256 by 192

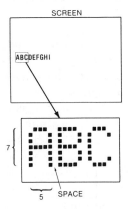

Fig. 5-2. Character representation by a 5-×7-dot matrix.

pixels or the corresponding character positions of about 40 characters per line by 24 lines. Monitors eliminate the "front-end" electronics and can display more pixels without smearing, or running together of adjacent pixels.

If you are looking for as much resolution as you can get in graphics, therefore, stay away from microcomputers that offer output only to a standard television. However, before you do that, read the following discussion on processing pixels.

PROCESSING PIXELS

When are 1024 by 1024 pixels too many? What is the optimum number of pixels to have in high-resolution graphics? Before you say as many as possible, let us discuss some of the implications of having a large number of pixels, another way of saying high resolution.

Memory

First, the greater the number of pixels, the more memory required. If the pixel is black and white only, then one *bit* can be used to represent the "on/off" status. One *byte* of memory contains 8 bits, so in a black and white display, divide the number of pixels required by 8 to find the amount of memory required. A

640-by-200 display in black and white would require 128,000 divided by 8, or 16,000 bytes of memory!

The memory used for the display has to come from somewhere. In some computers, such as the Apple II and Radio Shack Color Computer, it comes directly from the *random-access memory* (RAM) that is also used to hold user programs and data. In other computers, such as some graphics boards for S-100 systems, the *video display memory* is a separate memory that does not occupy precious user RAM.

The memory storage problem is further complicated by color graphics. Now instead of a single bit for the "on/off" of each pixel, we need to specify a color. Two bits hold coding for 4 colors, 3 bits coding for 8 colors, 4 bits coding for 16 colors, and so forth. RAM memory used in an 8-color mode in a 400-by-300 resolution system, therefore, would be 40,000 bytes, close to the available RAM in some systems. In many systems, the greater the resolution, the fewer colors that may be displayed.

Be aware, then, that the higher resolution and more colors that are provided in a high-resolution system, the more RAM memory that will be required. The ultimate system would offer many colors in high resolution without occupying user RAM area. Table 5-1 gives some specifications on memory required for various resolutions and colors. It assumes that each pixel is separately programmable as to color.

Processing Time

Another aspect of high-resolution graphics that is usually overlooked is the processing time required for high resolution.

The TRS-80® Model I has 128 elements by 48 elements, for a total of 6,144 black and white graphics elements. The IBM Personal Computer has 640 by 200 pixels in the high-resolution monochrome mode, for a total of 128,000 pixels. The IBM has 20 times the number of pixels, which is excellent for displays, but means that the processing will take roughly 20 times as long in many cases.

Table 5-1. Memory Requirements
for Graphics Resolutions

	(TYPICAL) MEMORY REQUIRED (BYTES)*			
RESOLUTION	MONOCHROME (1 BIT/PIXEL)	4-COLOR (2 B/P)	8-COLOR (3 B/P)	16-COLOR (4 B/P)
128 × 96	1,536	3,072	4,608	6,144
128 × 128	2,048	4,096	6,144	8,192
256 × 192	6,144	12,288	18,432	24,576
256 × 256	8,192	16,384	24,576	32,768
400 × 400	20,000	40,000	60,000	80,000
512 × 512	32,768	65,535	98,304	131,072
640 × 200	16,000	32,000	48,000	64,000
1024 × 1024	131,072	262,144	393,216	524,288

*Assumes "best case"
storage

Many versions of BASIC will process on the order of 200 points (pixels or groups of pixels) per second. This means that it would take about 15 seconds to fill half of a 6,144-element screen with random points or about 320 seconds to fill half of a 128,000-element screen! One obvious conclusion that can be drawn from this comparison is that high-resolution graphics is much more dependent upon good graphics processing software, either built into the BASIC provided with the system or as a separate applications package.

BASIC GRAPHICS COMMANDS

Let us take a look at some typical graphics commands that are available. We would find these on the IBM Personal Computer, the TRS-80 Color Computer, and other high-resolution graphics systems. They are illustrated in Fig. 5-3.

LINE lets the user draw a line between any two points on the display. It can also be used to draw a box outline or a filled-in box with the opposing corners of the box defined by the two points.

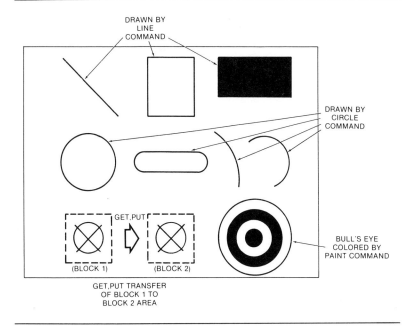

Fig. 5-3. Typical BASIC graphics commands.

CIRCLE draws a circle, ellipse, or arc on the screen. The figure may be of any size, from a single pixel to the limits of the screen size.

DRAW draws a series of line segments in 45-degree increments. The line segments can be any length or color and may be rotated or scaled in different sizes.

PUT and *GET* define graphics portions of the screen and enable saving them and redisplaying them in different areas at a later time.

PAINT colors a designated area of the screen in any specified color.

In addition to the above commands, there are other commands to set various graphics modes, define colors, and select the areas of memory available for graphics screens. These commands are very powerful and rapid (dozens of lines per second), are contained in the ROM, and make high-resolution graphics a great deal easier to use.

ADVANCED GRAPHICS APPLICATIONS

The simple commands that we have been discussing are primitive commands that will draw lines, simple shapes, and perform other rudimentary operations. What is involved in creating detailed charts, graphs, and pictures?

Again, this is where applications software is important. Even though the graphics commands available with current systems are powerful in terms of what existed several years ago, a great deal of programming is required to do something useful with them. Even more programming is required for those systems that provide only the hardware graphics capabilities and do not have the rudimentary graphics commands in ROM.

In general, it is fairly easy to produce colorful pie charts, line graphs, and simple plots of mathematical functions. Even if you do the programming yourself for these applications, it should be possible to produce some displays that will make your investment in graphics seem worthwhile.

The difficulty, however, lies in producing the types of displays that most people buy high-resolution graphics for. Let us face it, we have all seen the fascinating full-color, animated, three-dimensional displays that are used in the Hollywood science-fiction films. This type of display is the most difficult to produce.

Think about the steps that are necessary to generate a three-dimensional display:

- Determine the viewing angle.
- "Clip off" the area outside of the field of view.
- Determine which surfaces are in the foreground and which are further back from the viewing angle.
- Draw the surfaces with hidden lines deleted.
- Color and shade the surfaces.

These steps involve a great deal of trigonometric processing for a large number of points and sophisticated techniques for determining angles of view, hidden lines, and so forth. To create an animated three-dimensional display on a "real-time" basis is not only beyond the speeds of small computers, but probably beyond the capabilities of most large computing installations. As you might guess from such processing problems, there are few, if any, graphics software packages that will let you create spectacular Hollywood-type displays.

There are, however, software applications programs that will let you create simple stick-figure animated displays and full-color detailed pictures for high-resolution systems. In some cases the detailed pictures can be read in rapidly from disk to create animated effects, but do not expect the destruction of the Death Star.

CRITERIA FOR HIGH-RESOLUTION GRAPHICS

Now that we have somewhat of an overview of graphics, let us look at some of the other considerations in selecting a graphics system.

Graphics Modes

Most systems offer several different modes for display of graphics data. The most basic is usually straight text mode in which alphanumeric characters can be displayed in normal size, expanded size, or as a reverse (black lettering on a white background). Several graphics modes will probably also be offered in different degrees of resolution. The number of colors provided will probably decrease as the higher-resolution modes are reached. The highest resolution mode may be only a two-color mode.

Check system specifications carefully to see which modes provide for programmability of every point. In some modes, adjacent points must be identical colors, cutting down on the effective resolution of the display. Also determine whether you can live with predefined color "sets." It is rather hard to draw a portrait of the programmer as a young man with only green, yellow, blue, and red unless your subject is out of breath.

If you are interested in as much detail as possible, choose a system with high resolution and bear in mind that you will have to sacrifice RAM memory (in most cases) and processing time.

Mix of Alphanumerics and Graphics

Some systems provide either alphanumeric display or graphics display but not both at the same time. Other systems allow intermixing both alphanumerics and graphics. It is probably always desirable to have a system that will allow you to embed text in your graphics displays. If graphics displays do not allow text data, you may define text characters as graphics shapes and intermix them anyway. This is easy to do in some systems (as with a DRAW command) and harder to do in others.

Definable Graphics

Some systems allow you to use a standard character set for alphanumeric characters and also allow you to select a second or infinite number of character sets that are defined by the user. This is an excellent feature for generating non-English character sets such as Kata-Kana, Farsi, or other foreign or special character sets.

Outboard Graphics

In some cases, older microcomputers may be upgraded to higher resolution or color. There are various "outboard" devices that attach to the existing microcomputer system and generate the displays. These generally work well from a hardware standpoint, but may not have the necessary support software to enable you to easily interface without writing special *driver* programs.

S-*100* systems generally have the widest range of high-resolution graphics products available. Special S-100 graphics boards can be added as plug-in modules to existing S-100 systems without major problems (early S-100 boards had severe compatibility problems in some cases when boards from different manufacturers used conflicting signal lines).

If you are interested in black and white and shades of grey, you will find such equipment in S-100 plug-in boards. Typical boards would offer 256 shades from white to black and 65,536 points. The pictures generated by such graphics are extremely realistic.

Graphics Printers

Suppose that you have a detailed high-resolution display on your screen. Can you save it for posterity, short of getting out the trusty Minolta? Fortunately, the answer today is yes. A large number of graphics printers will print every dot of the screen display and do it at low cost.

A typical example of this is the Radio Shack Line Printer VII, which will print a line of 480 pixels at a spacing of 60 pixels per inch horizontally and a vertical spacing of 63 pixels per inch for under $400. This will reproduce any two color mode display exactly as it appears, except for a minor discrepancy in the aspect ratio.

The NEC Spinwriter is another example of a printer that will reproduce graphics data. It can be programmed to print a dot every 120th inch horizontally and every 48th inch vertically. Other related character printers (Diablo, Qume, Radio Shack) offer the same order of resolution.

Many other manufacturers offer *dot-addressable* printers that can be used to print graphics data from a video display or of other types.

Monitor Outputs

It was mentioned earlier that a television-type output cannot provide the resolution of a monitor-type output. There are two such monitor outputs. One is called *NTSC,* and the other RGB. The *National Television System Committee* (NTSC) output is a composite video signal with a single connector; this composite video can go into a color monitor and provide a much sharper display than a television-type output. The NTSC output can also be fed into an inexpensive ($20 to $30) modulator that will convert it to a television signal that can be received on channel 2 or 3. Although the resultant signal is again limited in resolution, the NTSC output is a way to eventually upgrade via a monitor to better resolution without changing the computer system.

The ultimate video output is the *RGB* or *red-green-blue* type. This is actually a set of three outputs that feed into the monitor but provide even better definition than the NTSC signal.

If you decide to use the modulated television receiver approach, or if your system has only this type of output, even inexpensive television receivers should be adequate; it is not necessary to buy the "top-of-the-line" television, as display quality will not be improved that significantly.

Digitizing Data

One problem with high-resolution graphics: Where do you get the picture to display? Handcrafting a picture is laborious. There is very little in the way of small computer digitized data bases although various government and industry computer departments are "digitizing the world." (Quite literally—they are converting natural and cultural features, such as buildings and man-made objects, into x,y,z coordinates in digital form!) Unfortunately, there are no low-cost automatic digitizers that will convert a picture into digital display data, with the exception of a few S-100 modules that will digitize a television picture. Hang in there, though. With the advent of high-resolution graphics, inexpensive digitizers will not be far behind!

Game-Oriented Displays

As you might expect, Atari (Atari 400 and 800) has excellent graphics hardware for games. However, to take maximum advantage of this graphics hardware requires programming at an assembly-language level. Although this is a subjective comment, I would say that between game machines and personal computers, the best game displays will be generated by the game machines. Again, game displays generated by BASIC programs are simply not fast enough for interesting games; assembly-language must be used.

RESOLVED: DON'T BE ENTRANCED BY GRAPHICS

I hope I have not been too cynical in the previous descriptions. High-resolution graphics can create some fantastic displays that can be very useful in business presentations and games alike. Study the characteristics of the graphics system carefully, using the above categories as guidelines, but remember to be a pragmatist in your selection of high-resolution hardware. Don't be like the vice-presidents of that aircraft company!

More Hardware for Your System

We have discussed the central processing portion of microcomputer systems, RAM memory, cassette tape, floppy and hard disks, line printers, and high-resolution graphics in the preceding chapters. Are there any other pieces of hardware that will make your system more valuable? Does an Apple computer use a 6502? Does Atari have game packages? Does IBM have computer experience? You do not think the manufacturers are going to sell you that basic system and then let you go without a fight, do you? There is an abundance of additional hardware that you can buy for your system, some of it useful and some not so useful. Let us talk about some of the additional devices you can buy in this chapter—a kind of hardware potpourri.

PLOTTERS

One of the more interesting peripheral devices to appear is the *plotter*. Plotters are very simple in concept, as shown in Fig. 6-1. They consist of either a *flatbed* that holds a piece of plotting paper or a surface over which a roll of paper moves. The marking device used to draw lines on the paper is a simple ink pen; it may be a graphics type, such as technical illustrators use, or a basic ball-point pen, depending upon the plotter. Some plotters also provide a choice of more than one color of ink.

The action of the pen is very simple; it either moves down, to contact the paper, or up, to a position above the paper. Depend-

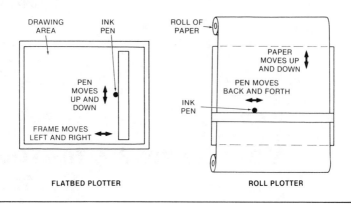

Fig. 6-1. Plotter operation.

ing upon the system, the pen also may move across the paper and in a vertical direction or across the paper with the paper moving in a vertical direction, as shown in the figure.

How far does the pen move? The beauty of the plotter is that the pen can move in very small steps, typically in hundredths or thousandths of an inch. The pen moves in a horizontal or vertical direction, but any angle of line can be created by moving the pen with both a horizontal and vertical component.

Because the step size is so small, virtually any line can be drawn by joining together a series of line segments, as shown in Fig. 6-2. The eye integrates these tiny line segments into a smooth line, even though at a microscopic level the line segments would appear as a series of right-angled lines.

Because the plotter may move in any of four directions (the paper or pen can back up) and because the pen can be lifted off the paper at will, virtually any figure can be drawn by the proper sequence of commands.

Sounds too good to be true, doesn't it? As you might have guessed, there are some disadvantages to plotter use.

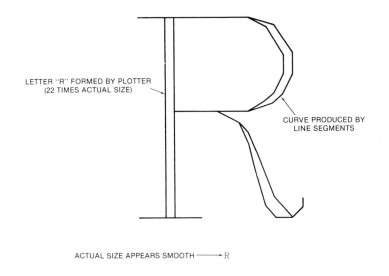

LETTER "R" FORMED BY PLOTTER
(22 TIMES ACTUAL SIZE)

CURVE PRODUCED BY
LINE SEGMENTS

ACTUAL SIZE APPEARS SMOOTH ──────► R

Fig. 6-2. Plotter line drawing.

First of all, it takes a relatively long time to draw a complex figure. The pen moves at 2 to 3 inches per second for inexpensive plotters. A bar graph consisting of 10 bars across an area of about 8 by 5 inches would take about 46 seconds to draw, and that is just the skeleton outline of the graph, without any filled-in areas.

Second, it takes a lot of programming to have the plotter do anything useful. In some cases the manufacturer supplies a software package to drive the plotter and enable the user to easily draw bar graphs, other plots, and geometric figures. In other cases you must program the plotter yourself.

Newer models of plotters, however, are intelligent. They do many functions automatically, under control of a built-in microprocessor. Here is a good example:

Radio Shack has an inexpensive plotter called the CGP-115 for its TRS-80 line (or any RS-232C or Centronics-port computer).

This plotter is a four-color plotter that uses four pens with red, blue, green, or black ink, instantly selectable under program control. The plotter will plot in either graphics or text mode. In the text mode, it will draw a complete ASCII character set with programmable character sizes.

In the graphics mode, the plotter can draw a line between any two points, change the color, move between any two points (pen off paper), rotate the print direction through 90-degree increments, draw an axis (with tic marks), draw dotted lines, and return to the origin, to name some of the commands.

Paper size is 4½ inches wide by 180 feet long. Ten years ago such a plotter in a larger version cost tens of thousands of dollars. The CGP-115 is about $250!

GRAPHICS TABLETS AND DIGITIZERS

Another interesting device is the *graphics tablet*. This is basically a pad that is about 8½ by 11 inches upon which a piece of paper is placed. The pad has an accompanying pen that moves across the surface of the pad.

When the pen is moved across the tablet, its motion is tracked by the computer. The computer interfaces with the electronics of the tablet at a high rate (hundreds or thousands of times per second) and reads the position of the pen at every point.

You can see the usefulness of such a device. The graphics tablet can be used to trace over existing drawings and digitize the drawings, converting the shapes into x/y coordinates that can be processed by the computer. Some versions of graphics tablets also have a built-in ink pen to allow you to construct drawings "on the fly," digitizing the points as the drawing is made.

Although, again like the plotter, this seems like the ultimate tool, there are some problems accompanying the device. Software support may not provide the capabilities you are looking for, and you have to write your own software to process the points once they are stored in RAM memory, not a trivial task. You may even have to write some of the input drivers to read the x/y position.

Because BASIC is fairly slow, the overhead of BASIC software supporting the graphics tablet may cause some points to be missed when data is read into the system. An assembly-language version of the input driver would solve the problem of acquiring the points but is beyond the capabilities of many users.

Again, though, the price of graphics tablets has been cut at least by 75% over comparable units several years ago. Graphics tablets can now be purchased for hundreds of dollars that will give a resolution of dozens of points per inch.

Graphics tablets are really digitizers that translate an x/y coordinate into digitized form suitable for storage in a computer memory. There are other digitizers that do not use the tablet approach but simply convert x/y position from any surface by a "sliding rod" or pantograph approach.

LIGHT PENS

Light pens are devices that read areas on video displays. These devices look like a fountain pen (anybody remember those?) with an electrical lead coming out of the top as shown in Fig. 6-3. The pen contains a *photodiode* or *phototransistor* device in the tip. These are light-sensitive devices that send a signal back to the computer. When no light is detected by the device, a 0 *bit* is read. When light strikes the device, a 1 *bit* is read.

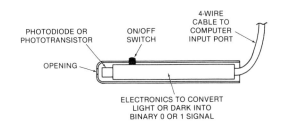

Fig. 6-3. Light pen operation.

When the light pen is in use, a software driver program continually reads the output of either 0 or 1.

Imagine a completely black screen with no display. When the light pen is held to the screen, the output will be continuous 0's as the software driver program reads the output at thousands of times per second.

Now suppose that the four spots are flashed on and off by a BASIC program at alternate times. Typically, the spots might flash on and off dozens of times per second and appear to be continuous spots to the eye.

It is important to note that each spot is controlled by the program and that one spot is on, followed by the next, and so forth. Only one spot is on at a time. If the light pen is held up to one of the spots, the light pen output will go from 0 to 1 whenever the spot is on. Since the BASIC program knows when the spot is on, it can detect which spot the light pen is at by noting when a 1 is read.

The light pen, therefore, can detect different areas of the screen and can be used to select menu options, digitize points, or perform other functions. In the most advanced form, a light pen is tied into the display electronics and can detect very small points on the screen. In most microcomputer applications, the light pen is used to select coarser areas of the screen because there is no way to modify the display electronics.

Since the light pen must be driven by software, the problem with this device is again in providing a comprehensive software driver.

REAL-TIME CLOCKS AND CONTINUOUS TIME/CALENDAR

A real-time clock is used inside a computer system's electronics to keep track of elapsed time. The usual form of such a device is an electronic circuit that monitors the power-line frequency of 60 hertz (60 cycles per second). Every $1/60$ of a second the computer system gets an *interrupt,* which results in an internal software counter being incremented by one count.

If the system is turned on at 12:00 noon, for example, the real-time clock counter would have 216,000 counts in it by 1:00 p.m.

Because the power line frequency is very accurate (it is used to drive synchronous motors that are found in most electrical clocks), the computer can accurately keep track of time.

When the computer system is shut off, however, the time must be reinitialized by entering a new time and date. Is there any way to maintain a continuous track of time? One option is the Hayes Stack Chronograph. This device is connected to the computer RS-232C port and runs independently of the computer system, keeping track of time and calendar date. The chronograph displays the time and date as well on a liquid crystal display. You might look upon it as a digital clock with a computer interface.

There are other comparable units and all can be used to enable your computer system to perform in real time, even to the extent of dialing up communications services and getting stock quotations together with some additional communications devices discussed in a later chapter!

OTHER HARDWARE DEVICES

The most common optional hardware device for small computers is the *modem* or modulator/demodulator. This device translates binary ones and zeroes into two different audio tones. When the audio output is fed into a telephone interface, your computer system can be used to communicate to other computer systems over phone lines, providing access to bulletin boards and other communications systems. Full coverage to this device is given in Chapters 13 and 14 when data communications and modem hardware and software are talked about.

It is also possible to connect *voice synthesizers* to your system to allow it to respond in voice, or to connect *voice recognition* hardware. These interesting peripheral devices are covered in Chapter 15.

Last, there are numerous devices that will interface your computer system to the outside world, ranging from the BSR electrical controller system to special purpose devices that will read remote temperature, burglar alarms, or turn your sprinklers on and off; those are covered in Chapter 16.

Look to see many more low-cost peripherals that will be hardware options for your computer system; we will be seeing more decreases in price and increases in intelligence in this area thanks to microprocessors!

Section

2

Software — Existing Tools and Writing Your Own

Languages — How To Talk to a Computer

BASIC is the universal language of the microcomputer world. BASIC has become so much a part of computers that it is easy to picture Remington-Rand engineers keying in BASIC test programs for the Univac I back in the 1950s. 'T aint so. BASIC wasn't always around. And yet it's hard to imagine an Apple, PET, TRS-80, or Xerox personal computer without BASIC as the primary language. Why? How did BASIC gain such a foothold in personal computers? Is it really as simple as represented? What other languages can be used with your computing system? Should they be used in place of BASIC?

This chapter attempts to provide some of the answers to those questions. In doing so, you will get a brief history of computer languages and thumbnail sketches of the currently popular microcomputer languages.

TWENTY-FIVE YEARS OF THE SAME INSTRUCTIONS

Microcomputer hardware remains remarkably unchanged from the earliest digital computers. Oh sure, we have taken gigantic steps in miniaturization—we have reduced several rooms of relays or vacuum tubes down to a postage-stamp sized chip. We have also made the same hardware less expensive by a factor of 1,000 or so and made the same advances in reliability. Lest I be tarred and feathered with computer printouts, let me hastily explain that I'm not discounting the work of countless computer design engineers. However . . .

If you look at computer instruction sets, you will find many of the same things accomplished by the Z-80 microprocessor in a TRS-80 or S-100 system or the 6502 microprocessor in the Apple or PET as were accomplished in the logic components of the Ferranti Mark I that Alan Turing programmed back in the 1950s. You will find instructions to add two numbers, instructions to load an accumulator from memory, instructions to store an accumulator to memory, and so forth. About the most complex instruction that can be executed by the microprocessor in your personal computer is one: to multiply two numbers; or two: to search a list of numbers for a given number.

Every program, whether it is VisiCalc or Adventure, ultimately resolves down into execution of hundreds of thousands or millions of these rudimentary *machine-language* instructions.

To be very unkind, today's computers (and all digital computers) are not much more than extremely fast adding machines or calculators with the ability to store data and instructions and to change the sequence of instructions.

MACHINE-LANGUAGE PROGRAMMING— BINARY ONES AND ZEROES

Initially, digital computers were developed and funded to solve number-crunching problems rapidly, such things as artillery trajectories, flight simulation, and enigma code breaking. The instruction sets of the early computers on up to current microprocessors reflect this arithmetic processing bias.

The most basic language is the numeric language of binary ones and zeroes, making up the *operation codes* that the microprocessors recognize as legitimate machine-language instructions. Let us look at a simple example. Suppose that we want to add the numbers from 1 to 100. In Z-80 machine language (S-100 systems, TRS-80 Models I, II, III, Apple Softcard, Northstar, and others), we would have the program shown in Fig. 7-1.

	Step	Instruction
00100001 00000000 00000000	1	Load total register with 0
00000001 00000000 01100100	2	Load current number register with 100
00001001	3	Add current number register to total register
00001101	4	Subtract 1 from current number register
00100000 11111100	5	If current number register not 0, back to 3

Fig. 7-1. Machine-language program to add the numbers from 1 to 100.

The actual program is made up of the five machine-language instructions on the left. Each instruction is shown in binary representation of ones and zeroes, the way it would appear in the memory of the microcomputer.

Of course, the programmer did not just sit down and write out the strings of ones and zeroes but wrote down a list of instructions from the instruction set of the machine as shown in the right-hand portion of the figure and then translated them into the equivalent machine-language codes, referencing a table of codes for the machine.

You can see that this language is extremely tedious. Since many instructions reference other instruction locations in the memory inserting or deleting instructions would require laborious hand translation of large portions of the program. For this reason, *assembly language* was developed very early in the computer game.

ASSEMBLY LANGUAGE—SYMBOLIC REPRESENTATION OF INSTRUCTIONS

Assembly language is a symbolic representation of machine-language instructions. Instead of writing down "load the total register with 0" and then manually converting this instruction to its binary form of 00100001 00000000 00000000, the programmer writes down "LD HL,0". An *assembler program* then takes the symbolic (text) form of the instructions and automatically translates it into the machine code of ones and zeroes. The same program to add the numbers from 1 to 100 is shown in assembly language in Fig. 7-2.

```
        LD    HL,0       ;LOAD TOTAL WITH 0
        LD    BC,100     ;LOAD CURRENT WITH 100
LOOP    ADD   HL,BC      ;ADD CURRENT TO TOTAL
        DEC   C          ;CURRENT-1 TO CURRENT
        JR    NZ,LOOP    ;GO IF CURRENT NOT 0
```

Fig. 7-2. Assembly-language program to add the numbers from 1 to 100.

Assembly language is much more readable and efficient than the machine-language version. We have let the computer do most of the work in the assembler program, replacing the tedious manual translation. Of course, the first assembler program for every machine is written in machine language! There is no assembler to assemble the assembler program! (Truthfully, although this was true on early computers there are now *cross-assemblers* to assemble programs from one microprocessor to another.)

ENTER FORTRAN

FORTRAN was one of the first high-level languages. Assembly language made programming much easier for early computer users. The computer, however, was still usable only by the computer scientist; one who was intimately familiar with the instruction sets of the computers and who felt comfortable with binary ones and zeroes and specialized *algorithms* (procedures) to process data.

FORTRAN (FORmula TRANslator), developed by IBM in the late 1950s, increased the base of users of computers by translating mathematical formulas. Instead of the essentially one-for-one translation of symbolic instructions into machine language, it took a mathematical formula and translated it into machine-

90

language code *sets*. This type of translation was called *compiling*. With the advent of FORTRAN, the engineer or scientist who was not intimately involved with computers could use a computer to solve sophisticated mathematical problems. The same programming problem shown in the earlier figures is shown in FORTRAN in Fig. 7-3.

Fig. 7-3. FORTRAN program to add the numbers from 1 to 100.

```
   TOTAL = 0.
   DO 20 I = 1,100
20 TOTAL = TOTAL + I
```

The assembler was an order of magnitude less tedious than machine-language programming. The FORTRAN *compiler* was another order of magnitude easier than the assembler. For this reason, compiler languages are termed *high-level languages*. The FORTRAN statements, while not English language, at least were very similar to mathematical formulas, and the engineer and scientist were able to learn the language without becoming intimately familiar with the computer system.

COBOL AND BUSINESS APPLICATIONS

In 1952, a Remington-Rand Univac I got national exposure in tabulating projections on the presidential election. The potential for computers in business data processing was publicized by Remington-Rand and other computer companies. One of the impediments to use of computers in business, however, was the translation process from accounting terms to a form that the computer system could understand. COBOL (COmmon Business Oriented Language) language made the translation more convenient.

COBOL was developed about 1960 specifically for business use. Like FORTRAN, it was originally developed as a *compiler*; a translator that would take each COBOL function and translate it into many machine-language instructions.

COBOL was more English-like than other computer languages. As a matter of fact, in a somewhat more naive computer atmosphere, it was represented as a language that would make it possible for managers to do their own programming and dispense with those costly and cantankerous programmers. Alas, programming staffs and empires proliferated, but once again, the programmer was another step removed from the intricacies of the computer hardware.

Fig. 7-4 shows the same program that has been discussed in COBOL, a rather unfair comparison, as COBOL is least efficient in number crunching.

```
130  PROCEDURE DIVISION
135  PGM-BEGIN. MOVE ZEROS TO TOTAL-COUNT,INC.
140  LOOP. IF INC IS GREATER THAN 100
150         GO TO PGM-END.
160      ADD 1 TO INC.
170      ADD INC TO TOTAL-COUNT.
180      GO TO LOOP.
190  PGM-END. STOP RUN.
```

Fig. 7-4. COBOL program to add the numbers from 1 to 100.

OTHER LANGUAGES IN THE 1960s

FORTRAN and COBOL remain two of the most popular and permanent languages on all types of computers. There were many other languages developed during this period, however, as the number of computer manufacturers and computer usage increased.

ALGOL (ALGOrithmic Language) was developed about 1960 primarily for mathematical processing. It is somewhat similar to FORTRAN in appearance. It was promoted by the Association for Computing Machinery (ACM) and used by hard-core computer scientists.

LISP (LISt Processing language) was developed in the early 1960s. LISP uses a *linked list* of data. Structures using LISP re-

92

semble binary trees. It remains a popular language among the devotees of artificial intelligence.

PL/1 (Programming Language 1) was developed in the late 1960s by IBM as a replacement for FORTRAN and COBOL. Although it gained some acceptance in large-scale data processing applications, it could not be called a success.

The list of other languages that were developed and even less successful than FORTRAN, COBOL, ALGOL, LISP, and PL/1 is enormous. This was the golden era of the language acronym, as evidenced by JOVIAL (Jules' Own Version of an International Algebraic Language), RPG (IBM's successful Report Program Generator), BOMP (Bill Of Materials Processor), DBOMP, SNOBOL, and many, many, others.

BASIC AND THE LANGUAGES OF THE 1970s

All the previous discussion takes us up to the 1970s. In the 1970s and before, minicomputers began to make their appearance. Minicomputers were physically smaller and much less expensive computer systems. Advances in semiconductor technology led to computers with fewer and fewer components; all performing many more functions than the components of previous computer systems.

Minicomputers were cheap! During this era, the minicomputer manufacturers did not offer much in the way of support software, certainly no higher-level language compilers. About all users got for their money were inexpensive pieces of hardware delivered in the dead of night and thrown on their doorstep. If they were very lucky, perhaps an assembler was included . . .

The culmination of packing more and more functions into a semiconductor chip was a complete microprocessor—a computer on a chip. The Intel 8080 microprocessor chip was one of the first of the 8-bit microprocessors, followed by the 6800 and 6502.

A small company in Albuquerque developed the first widely marketed personal computer, the MITS Altair 8800, built around the 8080 microprocessor. Initial sales were much better than expectations. Although at first the Altair 8800 had no assembler, an assembler and BASIC interpreter were soon implemented.

Why BASIC?

BASIC had been around for a number of years when MITS brought out the Altair 8800. Originally developed by John Kemeny and Thomas Kurtz at Dartmouth College, BASIC was intended primarily for use by computer science students. The acronym BASIC stands for *Beginner's All-purpose Symbolic Instruction Code* and indeed was more English-like than most previous languages and simple to use.

The BASIC developed for the Altair was implemented by Bill Gates, a principal in Microsoft. In contrast to most earlier high-level languages, it was an *interpretive* BASIC, rather than a compiler. Interpreters read in the language text, do some preliminary processing, but largely reprocess the text in each line every time the program is run. A compiler, on the other hand, compiles each statement into compact machine-language form, and this form of the program is run.

There are advantages and disadvantages to each. In general, a compiler is suited for programs that must run at the fastest speed or for program development on a large system shared by many programmers. An interpreter, on the other hand, runs more slowly (typically 10 or 20 times) than a compiler, but is very *interactive* (good machine and user communication) and ideally suited for a small, single-user system.

Altair BASIC turned the Altair from a machine that could run only hand-assembled machine-language programs into a truly useful machine. Microsoft soon produced BASIC interpreters for other microcomputer manufacturers many of which were created in the wake of the success of MITS.

As a matter of fact, Microsoft BASIC has become a popular high-level personal computer language. Microsoft has produced BASIC interpreters for most of the current personal computer systems. Although the exact formats differ from system to system, Microsoft BASIC on all systems is very similar. Fig. 7-5 shows the same sample program in Microsoft BASIC.

<table>
<tr><td>

Fig. 7-5. BASIC program to add the numbers from 1 to 100.

</td><td>

```
100  T = 0
110  FOR I = 1 TO 100
120  T = T + I
130  NEXT I
```

</td></tr>
</table>

Other 1970 Languages

Almost all personal computer systems offer a BASIC interpreter, many of them Microsoft BASIC, and many permanently stored in ROM (read-only memory). In addition, some offer the tried-and-true FORTRAN and COBOL primarily because there is a large base of users who have familiarity with these languages.

There are other languages that are challenging BASIC, FOR-TRAN, and COBOL, however. One of these is Pascal, named as a tribute to the seventeenth century mathematician Blaise Pascal. It was developed in 1970 in Zurich, Switzerland, by Dr. Niklaus Wirth and has been adapted to microcomputers by the University of California, San Diego. Pascal has received a wide following in all types of computer systems and is being taught in many universities. Though not as popular as BASIC, it appears that Pascal will be a widely used language for some time. Fig. 7-6 shows the sample program in Pascal.

Other languages that have gained followings are FORTH (a stack-oriented interpretive language), PL/M (a version of PL/1 for microcomputers), C (a language used on the new UNIX operating system), and PILOT (a language even easier to learn than BASIC).

WHICH LANGUAGE IS BEST?

Now to the crucial question. Which language is best? As in many other areas, the answer to this question is very subjective. Let us take each of the languages discussed and comment on them. In this book generally acknowledged facts are differentiated from opinion.

Machine Language

This language is best left to very short code segments that are embedded in BASIC or other high-level languages. Anything

```
BEGIN
FOR   I: = 1 TO 100 DO
      BEGIN
         TOTAL: = TOTAL + I;
      END;
END.
```

Fig. 7-6. Pascal program to add the numbers from 1 to 100.

done in machine language can generally be done much easier in assembly language.

Assembly Language

Assembly language should be used over machine language to automatically assemble machine-language code. Assembly language is difficult to learn and tedious to use. Program development times are 5 to 20 times as long as the equivalent program developed in BASIC or another language. *Debugging* (finding program bugs or errors) is also much less straightforward than a higher-level interpreter. On the plus side, much significant software (word processors, high-speed games, data management software) is written in assembly language. Assembly language is up to hundreds of times faster than an interpretive language and 5 to 20 times faster than a compiler language.

Interpretive BASIC

Interpretive BASIC is the stock BASIC found in ROM or as a standard BASIC. Interpretive BASICs are easy to learn, offer great flexibility, and are very interactive. One can enter a program, execute it, pause, examine values and results, edit the program, run the program again, and repeat the process forever. Interpretive BASICs are an ideal program development tool. An enormous base of programs exists for BASIC. One big drawback is the slow speed in comparison to compiler BASIC. Choose this language as a beginning language.

Compiler BASIC

Compiler BASIC generally offers the same functions and capabilities as interpretive BASIC. Compiler BASICs are not interactive as are interpretive BASICs. Programs must be compiled in their entirety, debugged, recompiled, and so forth, making for longer development times. In many cases, compiler BASIC will occupy inordinate amounts of disk storage for a small system. On the plus side, a compiled BASIC program will run much faster than the equivalent interpretive BASIC program. An ideal situation not often found: Develop your program under interpretive BASIC and then compile the final version for high speed. Compiler BASIC is generally available on the more popular personal computers.

FORTRAN

FORTRAN served as a workhorse for many engineers and scientists and was excellent for engineering problems. Microcomputer versions are compilers and tend to use much disk storage. Personal opinion: Unless you have done FORTRAN programming in the past or have an existing base of FORTRAN programs, use Pascal. If you are running large system FORTRAN programs, do not expect them to run properly on your microcomputer.

COBOL

COBOL is probably the most widely used large system language. Again, a microcomputer COBOL compiler tends to eat up storage in disk and memory. Much business software can be implemented in BASIC in lieu of COBOL. Personal opinion: Use only if you have COBOL experience or have an existing base of COBOL programs. If the latter case, do not expect large system COBOL programs to run properly on your microcomputer.

Pascal

Pascal generally uses a large amount of memory and disk storage, unless you have a tiny version, which is somewhat limited in processing capability. Pascal is very flexible and excellent for engineering and scientific applications. The existing base of programs is not as large as BASIC but is growing. Pascal is harder to learn than BASIC, but once learned offers rapid program development although not as interactive as BASIC. Personal opinion: Learn BASIC first and then try Pascal.

Other Languages

FORTH is a stack-oriented language that offers high speed and flexibility. It is rather abstract and not a good beginning language. LISP is sometimes available but is also abstract and difficult to learn. C is similar to Pascal and appears promising although it is not available on most personal computers at present.

CONCLUSIONS

Although each personal computer language has not been discussed in detail, this chapter should give you some of the background of why certain languages are popular. Many times the reason is largely historical. Try your hand at BASIC first, since it is the standard language and then see which other languages suit your particular type of processing.

Operating Systems — the Software Workhorse of Your System

CP/M. Apple DOS. NEWDOS. LDOS. TRSDOS. Confused by Disk Operating Systems? Wondering whether or not to buy that personal computer with disk drives or one without? Maybe you have a small computer with cassette tape and would like to upgrade to floppy disk drives. Will disk drives really give you that much power? Or are they just an expensive option?

The capabilities of a small computer disk system are, to a large extent, determined by the *operating system* for the computer. In Chapter 3 the physical makeup of disk drives was discussed. In this chapter let us see how those disk drives can be utilized efficiently by an operating system. All operating systems for small computers today are *Disk Operating Systems,* usually abbreviated *DOS.* The disk drive offers a means to store large amounts of data and to access that data rapidly, without operator intervention.

EARLY DISK OPERATING SYSTEMS

During the early days of microcomputers (way back five years ago), disk operating systems performed very basic functions. For the most part, they really only loaded programs automatically. Over the years, however, operating systems have gotten more and more complex and have pretty much kept pace with the hardware advances.

When you buy a disk drive for your small computer system now, you will get a disk operating system on a diskette as part of the package with the disk drive or drives. The disk operating system will be written in assembly language and will be on a portion of the diskette. In other words, it will take up some of the tracks, making those tracks unavailable for storing any other data. If your diskette has a storage capacity of only 90,000 bytes, this may be significant, but generally, there is a large portion of the diskette remaining for other programs and data.

If you have more than one disk drive on your system, then only one drive has to hold a diskette containing the disk operating system, freeing up the second (or third or fourth) drive so that it can contain only a *data diskette*.

In case you are wondering why the disk operating system could not simply be loaded into computer RAM (random-access memory), freeing up an entire diskette for program or data storage: The disk operating system generally is larger than the size of the RAM. Portions of it must be read off of the DOS diskette as required. This is called *overlaying*, as one portion of the DOS program overlays a previous portion that is no longer needed.

Most DOS software loads automatically from the DOS diskette. This is called *bootstrapping*. (The term arises from the computer system "pulling itself up by its own bootstraps" when power is first turned on or when the system is reset.

DOS FUNCTION NUMBER 1: LOADING AND STORING PROGRAMS

The first and probably most important function that all DOS have is to provide an easy way to load programs. All you have to do to load a program from most DOS is to type the name of the program. To load a disk BASIC interpreter you might have the following dialog:

>READY

BASIC

The >READY is a DOS *prompt* message, indicating that the DOS is waiting for the next command. When the DOS reads in the BASIC entry that you have typed, it will search a table of *file names*, called a *directory* for the name and location (track, sector, number of sectors, and other information) of BASIC. It will then find the proper track and sector (there may be several segments) and load the program automatically in several seconds.

With some DOS, such as CP/M, you will automatically get a standard set of programs—an editor program, debug package, an assembler, a BASIC interpreter, and so forth. These will be on the DOS disk and can be called by simply typing the name. In other cases, you may have to add the programs to the DOS disk.

Once in the Disk BASIC interpreter, you can easily save BASIC programs that you create by a command such as

SAVE"MYPROG"

that will save a BASIC program called "MYPROG" on disk. The DOS will take care of all the functions of reading the program from RAM, storing it on a track or tracks, and creating a directory entry for the program name and location. Thereafter, "MYPROG" can be read from that diskette by entering a command such as

LOAD"MYPROG"

while in Disk BASIC.

DOS FUNCTION NUMBER 2:
LOADING AND STORING DATA FILES

The second most important function that DOS provides is the ability to store and read DATA files from BASIC or other programs. Within a BASIC program you can write a *record* on diskette. Look upon a *file* as being the complete telephone book for New Podunk, Wisconsin. The *record* would be the listing of Barden, William 250 N.S. MEMORY LANE 555-1212.

Involved BASIC programs might have many files—one for accounts receivable, one for payroll information. They would all be able to be created, updated, and read in seconds under DOS interaction with the BASIC interpreter. Since an unlimited number of diskettes could be used, the amount of data storage would be unlimited.

This *file-manage* capability is one of the most powerful features of disk operating systems. Files, whether they are program or data files, are automatically handled by the DOS. Entries are made in the directory, disk space is allocated, old entries can be deleted, and so forth. In some operating systems several different *file structures* may also be used—*sequential files*, where records are read from beginning to end; *random files*, where any record may be read without going through preceding records, and other more complicated types.

DOS FUNCTION NUMBER 3: FILE MAINTENANCE

Since file management constitutes a large portion of the DOS code and activity, each DOS has a number of commands that are directly related to disk files.

The disk file directory can be listed on the display or system line printer by a command such as

>READY

DIR (P)

that would list the directory files on the line printer. This is an obvious requirement for finding out which files are on diskette.

Files can be deleted by a bellicose KILL command, renamed by the command RENAME MYPROG TO HISPROG, copied from a diskette in one drive to a diskette in another drive with the instruction COPY MYPROG:0 TO MYPROG:1, or appended with the command APPEND MYPROG TO HISPROG.

102

Free space = 31.2K Drive 0 LDOS-5.0 — 10/13/81

Filespec Attributes Prot / LRL #Recs / Ext File Space Mod Date

Filespec	Attributes	Prot	/ LRL	#Recs / Ext	File Space	Mod Date
BOOT/SYS SIP	EXEC		/ 256	5 / 1 S =	1.2 K	
SYS6/SYS SIP	NO		/ 256	41 / 1 S =	11.2 K	01-Aug-81
SCRIPSIT/LC	ALL		/ 256	44 / 5 S =	11.2 K	13-Oct-81
ART1013/POP +	ALL		/ 256	70 / 1 S =	17.5 K	13-Oct-81
DIR/SYS SIP	READ		/ 256	10 / 1 S =	2.5 K	
SYS0/SYS SIP	NO		/ 256	17 / 1 S =	5.0 K	01-Aug-81
SYS8/SYS SIP	NO		/ 256	3 / 1 S =	1.2 K	01-Aug-81
SYS1/SYS SIP	NO		/ 256	5 / 1 S =	1.2 K	01-Aug-81
SYS2/SYS SIP	NO		/ 256	5 / 1 S =	1.2 K	01-Aug-81
SYS10/SYS SIP	NO		/ 256	3 / 1 S =	1.2 K	01-Aug-81
SYS3/SYS SIP	NO		/ 256	3 / 1 S =	1.2 K	01-Aug-81
SYS4/SYS SIP	NO		/ 256	5 / 1 S =	1.2 K	01-Aug-81

Fig. 8-1. Typical disk directory.

DOS FUNCTION NUMBER 4: UTILITY PROGRAMS

More powerful disk operating systems not only have the standard support software such as editors, assemblers, BASIC interpreters, and such, but they also have a number of utility programs. These are programs that perform important subordinate functions.

Utility programs are not part of the DOS itself, just as the support software is not in the DOS program but can be easily loaded from the DOS diskette.

All diskettes from the diskette manufacturer are, for all practical purposes, completely blank. They must be formatted by putting on a skeleton format that defines the track and sector locations and identification. The FORMAT utility performs this task.

Another utility provides a means to copy the entire diskette onto another diskette. All computers have voracious appetites for late evening snacks of magnetic material of all types, and a BACKUP utility ensures that a backup copy of important diskettes exists.

Other utilities allow *dumps* of files on diskettes for investigation, *patching* of diskette files, and other more esoteric functions.

DOS FUNCTION NUMBER 5: INPUT/OUTPUT HANDLING

One of the important functions of large-scale computer operating systems is to allow the programmer to handle input/output (i/o) to different devices in an easy manner. The programmer does not have to be concerned with how a line printer operates down on a nuts and bolts level. How a DOS does this for disk files was discussed earlier. Many of the more sophisticated systems also provide a means to *route* the data intended for one device to another device.

Suppose, for example, that you wanted a report that would normally be printed on a line printer to go to a disk file for later use. On some DOS, it is possible to route the line printer output to a disk file. Some DOS also *spool* the line printer output to a disk file and print during slack periods in system operation. This increases the overall efficiency and speed of the system.

CP/M and some other DOS allow the user to define his own device *driver*. This lets the user write a software driver for an odd peripheral device, such as an early model teletypewriter or a McHenry Pickle-Bottle machine.

Another feature found in CP/M and other DOS is the concept of *logical* and *physical devices.*

The *physical device* is the actual type of physical I/O device. A line printer might be designated LPT, and a video display CRT.

The *logical* device is the generic functional device, such as the listing device, designated LST.

The listing of a BASIC program might normally go to the listing device, LST. By suitable definitions, however, the LST device may be defined to be the line printer (LPT), the video display (CRT), a disk file, or the McHenry Pickle-Bottle machine (MPB).

Logical and physical devices actually preceded the idea of routing and are offshoots of large-scale operating systems.

DOS FUNCTION NUMBER 6:
AUTOMATIC SYSTEM OPERATION

Imagine giving your computer system instructions in the morning to load BASIC, load your accounts receivable program, run the accounts receivable by merging the latest transactions, print out a report, and then load and run a telecommunications program to automatically dial up and assemble stock market data —all without operator intervention!

It *is* possible. Some DOS have the capability to perform a *Job Control Language*, or JCL. The chief reason for implementing large-scale operating systems was to make efficient use of multimillion dollar computer systems by running many programming jobs concurrently. (See "Multiprogramming" next.) JCL allowed each programmer to define what operating system functions, such as assembly, FORTRAN compile, COBOL compile, applications program execution, and so forth, that were wanted.

In DOS with JCL, commands are entered by keyboard lines, they go into a disk file, and they are then executed one at a time without human intervention. If a large number of jobs are to be run, this feature can be very handy. For a single-user system with only occasional use, however, this is probably unnecessary.

MULTIPROGRAMMING

The discussion above described single-user systems. There are a number of disk operating systems that will run several jobs concurrently.

You could, for example, be compiling a FORTRAN program while running a BASIC inventory program. The advantage? During the huge (in microprocessor terms) amounts of time spent waiting for the next character to print on the line printer, a second or third task is executed. This *overlaps* computer program execution with line printer, disk, and other I/O and increases the total efficiency of the system.

In another type of operating system, a *background* job, such as a BASIC compilation could be run at the same time as a time-critical, real-time, *foreground* job, such as monitoring a nuclear reactor. The background job would be run after all pending foreground tasks have been processed (hopefully).

Still another type of operating system would handle a time-sharing system, servicing many users over a telecommunication system.

All three advanced types of operating systems exist for some small computers. For most small computer system users, however, the less sophisticated, single-user operating system is more than adequate.

SHOULD YOU USE A DOS?

In fact, this question really amounts to "should you use a disk drive with your system?" My personal feeling is that if you are attempting to do *anything* useful with your system, you should by all means be using a disk with the accompanying DOS. If you are using your system only as a learning tool or for occasional games, then a DOS system may be a luxury.

WHICH DOS IS BEST?

This question is easily answered for some small computer systems, because there may be only one DOS (or none) available. However, for microcomputer systems that sell in larger quantities, there may be several DOS available. The Radio Shack Model I system, for example, has the standard Radio Shack DOS, TRSDOS, plus NEWDOS, LDOS, DOSPLUS, and CP/M, in addition to others.

CP/M (Control Program/Monitor by Digital Research Inc.) has been adapted to a number of computers. Initially designed for S-100 systems, versions now run on Apple, Radio Shack, and other computers, in addition to current S-100 configurations, such as the Osborne 1. It is an extremely successful system and has a large amount of software available. Adapting it to a non-

S-100 system may pose some minor compatibility problems, however.

When multiple DOS are available for your system, use the same cautions as in buying other software—the size and stability of the manufacturer, support from the manufacturer, and adequate documentation. Also look for compatibility of the DOS with other systems. Some DOS will not allow diskettes generated by other DOS to be used, including the DOS from the original computer manufacturer!

Developing Your Own Software (or Please Pass the Aspirin)

So you want to be a programmer, eh? You are a staid, white-collar type who purchased a small computer system with the intent of running some business programs geared to your own ideas and business, and now you want to transform yourself into a competent programmer.

I have the answer for you, Dr. Jekyll. It is a magic elixir I just whipped up in my computer lab. It will transform you into Harry Hyde, Programmer Par Excellence. Away with the three-piece suit and button-down shirt and into a beard, plaid shirt, and jeans! Away with your middle-of-the road FM music and into Bach's Brandenburg Number 5! Away with the Angels game and into Brooks Vantage running shoes!

And now the only thing remaining is the *plan* . . . You must learn the secret of professional programmers . . . An ancient art . . .

In this chapter you will get some tips on developing your own software, whether you do it yourself or hire one of those bearded, frisby-throwing programmers to do it for you. And you will see the *plan*. The ancient formula of the programming art that heretofore has been cleverly concealed by the priesthood of computer scientists.

DO YOU REALLY NEED TO DO
YOUR OWN SOFTWARE?

However, before you even think about developing your own program, take a long, hard look at existing applications programs. Today there are probably ten times the applications programs there were two years ago. One ground rule that few people will dispute is that it is much more cost effective for you to buy an existing applications program for accounts receivable, inventory control, mailing lists, spread sheets, data management, and others than to develop your own. Whatever you have to pay, it is going to be much less expensive than the hundreds of hours required to write, or to have someone write, your own program.

Your first step, then, is to research the existing programs to see if any of them will perform the applications for you.

It is true that some of the applications programs are relatively rigid in format and will not let you convert your own manual methods to the program record or report format. However, look at the existing applications program and give some serious thought about just how difficult it would be to adapt to the program formats. In most cases, this will be a fraction of the time and expense of developing your own program.

Okay, you have done that, and there are not any existing programs that fit your needs. You are determined to produce your own program, tailored to your specific needs. Possible, certainly. Many people have done just that, and some have even done it a second and third time! How long, though, can you expect the program to take, and how much money will you have to invest in the program?

TWICE THE PROGRAM IS MORE THAN
TWICE THE TIME

Let us review some BASIC truths: Typical BASIC business programs range in size from 4,096 (4K) bytes to over 65,536 (64K) bytes in length. The size in bytes is the amount of random-access-memory (RAM) storage that the program occupies in the small computer. Some programs will have to be made up of several segments, which will have to be loaded into the RAM from the disk at different times.

Typical times to develop BASIC programs take from 100 hours to thousands of hours. The greater the size of the program, the slower the rate of the development. A program that is twice the size may take three or four times the time to develop.

Few programmers work for minimum wage. Competent BASIC or COBOL programmers in industry with several years of experience make $12 per hour or more. Why should they work for you for any less? Especially when you probably would not tolerate their frisby-throwing. Of course, you may be fortunate in finding a programmer who works in industry and wants to "moonlight" on a part-time job or a sharp college student who owns a small computer and has good practical experience, but expect to pay at least $12 per hour for competent programming help.

Putting the facts above together, we come up with a typical business applications program for a small computer at about $1,200 to $24,000 or more. Shocked? It *is* a shock, especially when you recall the computer store salesman with 96 teeth who laughingly told you that you could find thousands of programmers to program your computer for minimum cost.

"Dammit," you say, "I'll write the program myself! Who needs programmers, anyway? BASIC is . . . well . . . basic."

PROGRAMMING IT YOURSELF

My favorite book advertising blurb describes a beginner-level book on BASIC that promises to teach you how to program in "one or two days"! As you probably know by now, it is possible to be running some extremely simple programs in a few days, but how long does it take to become a reasonably efficient BASIC programmer capable of writing your own business programs?

Unfortunately, business programs require use of just about all the powerful BASIC commands for *arrays, string manipulation,* and *disk file manage.* There are probably 60 or 70 different commands involved, and considerable time is needed to learn their syntax (format) and functions. Once you know the general function and form of the commands, additional time is required to become proficient in their use. Writing programs for business is truly analogous to using a foreign tongue; you do not want to have to page through foreign-language phrase books to find the proper words—ideally they should come to mind almost automatically.

So it is with BASIC and other languages. To achieve the ability to speak fairly fluently in your computer language is going to require at least hundreds of hours.

In addition to learning the computer language of course, you are going to have to invest almost an equivalent amount of time in learning the idiosyncracies of your system—how to format and back-up diskettes, how to connect cables from the main computer to a printer, how to detect system errors, and so forth.

Now all of this is possible. I know many people who have started with no computer experience and have gone on to write huge programs that dramatically changed their business operation. At this point they are in an enviable position—they have invested the time and know computer technology and can apply that knowledge to other business problems. However, I must point out the other extreme; there are people who have tried to learn the new technology and failed. They are still dumbfounded by what others would consider simple concepts. And these are intelligent people. They simply are not "computer-minded," just as puts and calls, crummy trusts, writs of habeus corpus, disk-brake actuators, and Podocarpus Elongata baffle some of the computer whizzes.

WHAT, YOU STILL WANT TO DEVELOP YOUR OWN PROGRAM?

I can see that you are a tough customer. If you are still determined to write your own program, let us set out a procedure to follow. Even if a program is written for you, the programmer will probably follow these steps. This is the mysterious plan mentioned before.

The classic program development plan is

- A *design specification* is produced.
- The program is flowcharted.
- The program is coded.
- The program is debugged.
- The program is exercised.
- The final documentation is prepared.
- The program is run in parallel with existing systems and phased into operation.
- Occasional bugs are discovered and the program maintenance is done.

Design Specification

This is perhaps the most important phase of the program development cycle, and one that is usually neglected. The program design specification should describe in detail what the program will do. It should give all screen and report formats, including menus, operating procedures, error messages, estimated disk storage and speed requirements, and general theory of operation.

The design spec cannot be too detailed. If you have hired a programmer or programming firm to write the program for you, they should be able to define all of the above items. If they cannot, then consider finding one that can. Make them spell out how fast the program will operate and what the storage requirements will be; these are important aspects of the operation of the program.

The design spec also protects the programmer. A detailed design spec will prevent the "I thought the program was going to do this" syndrome on the part of the purchaser. It also prevents "creeping elegance" from rearing its inevitable head; additional program capabilities may require a great deal of redesign or recoding on the part of the programmer.

An addendum to the design spec might be a detailed *logical design specification* that the programmers might use to outline how they are going to accomplish the programming task. If you are doing your own programming, this is probably a necessity. It is also a good thing to have when the job is completed and the programmer has moved to Sri Lanka; other programmers can use it to expunge possible bugs that are found at a later time.

113

Program Flowcharting

The next step after the design spec is program flowcharting. There are those who will tell you that flowcharting is not necessary. They are partially right. For small programs, BASIC is excellent for *interactive development*. Flowcharts are not normally required in this case. I assume here, however, that we are talking about a moderate to large program, and for this size, some type of detailed logical description of program flow is necessary.

The typical flowchart uses not more than about a dozen symbols to represent program procedures, decisions, reports, disk activity, on- and off-page *connectors*, and so forth, as shown in Fig. 9-1. These symbols are somewhat standard but may vary from company to company and from programmer to programmer.

Some excellent programmers do not use flowcharts but list program steps in abbreviated form. Again, one advantage to having a flowchart is that it can be used later to correct program bugs. If you are writing your own program, definitely plan to use a flowchart until you discover another method of listing program flow that works as well.

Program Coding

Once the program has been flowcharted and checked, it can be *coded*. This involves translating the broad procedural steps of the flowchart into BASIC or other language commands. If the design spec and flowchart have been well done, this task goes fairly rapidly.

The result of the coding is a set of BASIC code representing the applications program. You may be horrified to see the result by the way. BASIC commands by themselves are readable and clear cut. However, when these commands are in a large program and the program has been reduced in size by combining commands on single lines, eliminating comments, and eliminating blank characters, which take up space in RAM, the result is largely unreadable as shown in Fig. 9-2.

If you are doing your own programming, you may want to use single commands per line and put in remarks and spaces to make

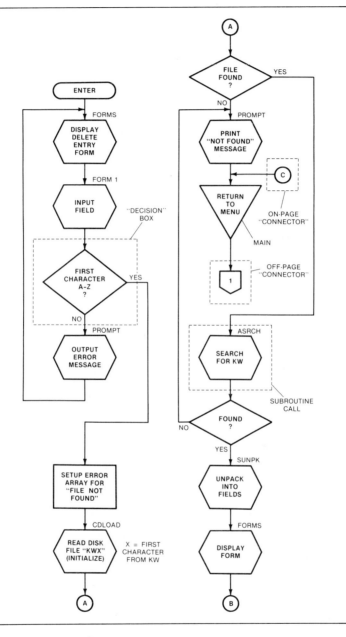

Fig. 9-1. Typical flowchart.

```
110  H$ = "0123456789ABCDEF"
120  LINEINPUT"
     FILESPEC: ";FS$:ONERRORGOTO9000:OPEN"I",1,FS$
125  ONERRORGOTO0:CLOSE:OPEN"R",1,FS$:SN = 0
130  FIELD1,255 AS D$
140  LINEINPUT"
     SECTOR NUMBER (OR 'ENTER' FOR NEXT SECTOR): ";S$
150  IFS$ = """"THENSN = SN + 1ELSESN = VAL(S$):IFSN<1THENCLOSE:GOTO100
160  GET1,SN:IFPEEK(14312)>127THENPRINT"LP NOT READY":GOTO 140
170  LPRINT" ":LPRINT"FILESPEC: "FS$;TAB(35)"SECTOR; "SN:LPRINT" "
```

Fig. 9-2. Typical BASIC code.

the BASIC program readable, and then compress the program
after it has been debugged.

Debugging

After coding, the program is debugged. This simply means that
program errors are ferreted out and corrected. Program debugging is usually a considerable part of most program development, possibly as much as 80% when *exercising* and *program
maintenance* are considered.

Exercising

Now for the second most neglected part of program development, program exercising. After debugging, obvious errors have
been corrected. However, at this point there are almost without a
doubt subtle (or not so subtle) bugs remaining in the program.
These errors are found by program exercising.

In most cases it is simply not possible to test all possible conditions that will come up in a program. There may be literally bil-
lions of combinations of input data, far too many to test in a
reasonable time. However, the program should be exercised with
as many different combinations of program functions and data as
feasible. Software development companies call this *alpha* and
beta test-site exercising; that is, various users run the software
package and note any failures.

116

Most programmers do not spend enough time in this phase of the software development cycle, for obvious reasons. It is drudge work and not cost effective for them.

Final Documentation

Once all the previous steps have been completed, the final documentation for the program is prepared. This will include any changes to the design spec and flowcharts. The most important part of this, however, is a final program version that has been adequately debugged and exercised. If you do not have this final program version, it will be extremely difficult to maintain the program at a later time. Of course in BASIC, the program will probably exist as a program file on diskette.

Running the Program in Parallel

The program is now ready to be run in parallel with existing methods. This amounts to entering the same data into the program as with manual methods or the current program and comparing the results. Do not throw that important data into the black abyss of the video display terminal until you are certain that the program is functioning properly. This may require days or even weeks of parallel operation.

Program Maintenance

In large programming installations in industry, more money is spent in program maintenance than in actual program development! It takes considerable time for a programmer to go back and correct errors or deficiencies in a program after the program has been officially released. This is true even if the same programmer maintains the program who wrote the program but is even more a factor when a different programmer is used for program maintenance.

Again, it is important to find program bugs during the program debugging and exercising rather than after the release of the program. Again, an adequate design spec, logical design spec, and flowchart are a necessity.

Will bugs appear in a program after it has been released? Almost certainly. Expect them and be prepared to pay somebody to fix them or spend the time yourself in program maintenance.

CHOOSING A PROGRAMMER

Maybe you have decided that you cannot take the time to do your own programming. How do you choose a programmer who can do the job?

There is a mystique about programmers. Video game companies have scenic retreats for programmers so that they can develop new products. Other companies lure programmers with stock options and extravagant fringe benefits. Programmers are caricatured as bearded, sandaled, frisby-throwing freaks. Are they really that different?

The ability to program cannot be easily categorized. Programming is neither a science nor an art; it is a combination of both demanding a high degree of creativity.

Some of the most successful programmers do not look like white-collar businesspeople (but some do!), and you may be making a mistake in choosing one the same way you do your insurance agent or stockbroker. Here are some general guidelines in choosing a programmer for your application. Those I consider most important are marked with an asterisk.

- What previous programming projects has he or she done?* As always, recommendations from previous clients are a good way to choose contractors.
- Is he or she familiar with your computer system?* There are many software houses that have done a great deal of work on larger computers, tend to discount smaller computers, and would not be as efficient on your small system. Don't pay for their education.
- Is he or she familiar with your language?* There is no point in hiring an expert COBOL programmer for a BASIC system.
- Is he or she willing to give you a detailed specification and flowchart?* Review the previous discussion for the reasons these are important.

- What will be the plan for exercising the program?* The programmer may really "sling code" but fail in the quality of the final product.
- Will he or she provide training for use of the program? If the program is to be used for unskilled office help who are intimidated by computers, this is an important requirement. Not everyone is as forward thinking as you.
- What academic background does he or she have? What professional societies does he or she belong to? Does the programmer have certification, such as a Certificate in Data Processing (CDP) or Certificate in Computer Programming (CCP)? There are many professional programmers who neither belong to professional societies nor have certification. However, practical experience and academic or professional credentials make an impressive combination.

Programmers are an independent breed. Learn to tolerate their quirks and you may get a better product. Work with them and you may learn some tricks yourself about program development. But take care in learning too much about programming lest you turn into Harry Hyde. The first indication is wondering how you would look with a mustache . . .

Tips on How To Buy Software

This is the story of the nonidentical twins, Trader Dick and his brother Rick. Dick and Rick were born during the same year that the first commercial computer, the Univac II, was introduced. Being products of the computer age, Dick and Rick both became small computer addicts, buying microcomputers with disk drives, and a full complement of peripherals during the early 1980s. Their interests ranged from home computer applications through data communications and into advanced business applications. Both started with about the same amount of computer hardware.

Trader Dick got his nickname because of his obsession. You see, his goal became to acquire as much software as humanly possible. And as cheaply as possible. Dick begged, borrowed, and traded software. Any type of software. He publicized his trading activities on computer bulletin board systems from coast to coast. He came into group meetings of users with his microcomputer loaded with blank diskettes and came out with another 20 programs or so. He had computer klatsches in his home with his cronies and picked up other programs. His "old-boy" network kept him informed of new products as they came out.

Rick, on the other hand, started with several hundred dollars, followed a well-planned approach to software evaluation, and made choices of a dozen or so software packages.

Rick could see the effect of the obsession Dick had almost from the start of his collecting. Dick was constantly complaining

121

about programs that did not run properly, lack of documentation, his inability to remember the procedures for running similar programs, and the problem of support from the software manufacturer.

Today, Dick is a derelict in the skid-row district of Silicon City, California, while Rick owns a Rolls Corniche, a yacht, and a Beech Baron. What was the difference? What made Rick successful in his computing avocation while his twin became a failure? The difference was the method of acquiring software. In this chapter, you are going to get some software analysis tips from Rick, excerpted from his book, "How I Turned $400 in Software into Three Million Dollars of Real Applications in My Spare Time."

THE NATURE OF SOFTWARE

Before you are let in on these secrets from Rick, though, let us take a brief look at the business of producing software.

To paraphrase the anecdote about the newspaper business, software is not produced to entertain, nor to provide a full complement of applications for computers, nor for other reasons; software is produced to make money for the software companies.

There are basically three types of software manufacturers, "garage-shop" developers, professional software houses, and computer manufacturers.

Garage-shop manufacturers are the small entrepreneurs who decide to produce a better mousetrap. Just as in other businesses, the small software developer runs the gambit from inexperienced to highly competent. Small manufacturers in general, however, are characterized by lack of capital, lack of distribution, inadequate documentation, and lack of software support once the shipment of the product is made. This is not to say that there are not garage-shop products that are not excellent.

Professional software houses are full-time operations employing from a few to hundreds or more people. They are in the business

122

of developing software packages for existing or newly designed computers. Software houses have been around since the early days of computers. There are now software houses that primarily develop software for microcomputers. One example of a highly successful software house is Microsoft, a Bellevue, Washington company that has cornered the market on BASIC interpreters and produces other software packages.

Some software houses operate almost exclusively with full-time permanent programmers within the company themselves. Many software houses, however, solicit programs from outside programmers, market the software for the programmer, and pay the programmer a royalty, typically 20% of the package.

Software houses are characterized by better capitalization, good quality control (testing of programs), good documentation, and customer support (to a certain extent).

Computer manufacturers initially had very little software for their products. Most microcomputer manufacturers now, however, are becoming software manufacturers as well, as users become more and more aware of the need for adequate software. The larger manufacturers have their own programming departments producing software for their machines; most manufacturers also buy software packages from outside programmers either on a lump sum or royalty basis.

Whether the software producer is a large or small company or computer manufacturer, there are several truths that are evident:

- Software is expensive to produce because of the sheer number of hours and the expertise required.
- Software is becoming highly competitive. Competition has the effect of producing better software for the user as external software companies compete with the software from manufacturers and each other.
- Software is tending to be more significant and powerful. The days of "50 short business programs" consisting of 10 lines of BASIC code each are ending.

Having looked briefly at some of the characteristics of software suppliers, let us look at some of the secret methods employed by Rick and others to make intelligent choices of software.

SOFTWARE TIP NUMBER 1:
SOFTWARE MAY NOT FOLLOW THE MACHINE

If you do not currently have a microcomputer and are thinking of buying one, don't fall for the ploy from the seller that "the software is bound to follow." The software may never follow. Software for a particular microcomputer is largely a function of how well the microcomputer sells. A system that sells hundreds of thousands of units is definitely going to have software, because it not only generates money to fund the software development of the manufacturer, but it also motivates the software companies to produce software for those hundreds of thousands of systems. Conversely, if the system does not do well, there will be a dearth of software.

These days, microcomputer companies are big business and have adequate backing. On the other hand there are many companies and some will have to fall by the wayside. Choose a system that has at least a reasonable number of units already sold and a moderate amount of existing software. Never buy the system on promised software. Even among existing companies with hundreds of thousands of systems sold, software production *slips* of six months are not uncommon—that is a release of software six months later than when it was promised!

SOFTWARE TIP NUMBER 2:
BUY AS FEW SOFTWARE PACKAGES AS POSSIBLE

One reason Rick succeeded while Dick failed was because of the number of software packages Dick had to contend with. It is difficult to learn to operate a few software packages efficiently, and almost impossible to remember the differences in input formats, output formats, commands, and options with a dozen packages that you use regularly. Generally it is better to buy one comprehensive software package, like VisiCalc or Wordstar, than to piece together several packages that collectively perform the same functions.

124

SOFTWARE TIP NUMBER 3:
BEWARE OF FREE SOFTWARE

Dick had diskettes and diskettes full of software, much of it originally free. Free software is generally like other free products. Some of it may be good, but most of it is marginally useful. The best software (in this free-enterprise system) comes from people who are trying to make a buck. Good software requires an enormous amount of programming time, typically hundreds or thousands of hours. It is hard to find someone sufficiently motivated to produce good, free software. Also, even if the software *is* good, chances are you will not find adequate documentation or manufacturer support for the software.

Much of the software published in magazines falls under the category of free software. If the software is *that* good, the programmer can probably make more money by selling it to software houses or manufacturers. Here again, there are exceptions. Some people write articles on their "labors of love" and produce excellent programs.

Two exceptions, among others, to magazine software are *Dr. Dobbs Journal* (all computers) and *The Alternate Source* (TRS-80 oriented), which have contained a great deal of well-written software including *Tiny BASIC* in the public domain.

SOFTWARE TIP NUMBER 4:
USE THE DOCUMENTATION AS A GUIDE

A software package may be excellent and have poor documentation. Very few poor software packages have excellent documentation. For that reason, look over the manual on the software to find out how the software package works. If the manual seems to be comprehensive, chances are the software package will work well. If the documentation is scanty, there is a good chance that the software, too, is poorly organized.

In many cases you will be able to buy the manual separately for more expensive software packages. In some cases, the manufacturer will allow the manual cost to be credited on the purchase of the software package if you should decide to buy.

SOFTWARE TIP NUMBER 5:
BUY PROGRAMS IN ASSEMBLY LANGUAGE NOT
HIGHER-LEVEL LANGUAGE

Assembly-language programs run from dozens to hundreds of times faster than their equivalent BASIC or other higher-level language counterparts. The most extreme case of the speed difference is when the program is written in *interpretive* BASIC: less extreme cases are *compiler* BASICs or other compiler-language versions.

Assembly-language versions of applications generally require less memory than versions in higher-level languages.

If you have a choice between an application written in BASIC and one written in assembly language, a good ground rule to follow is to choose the assembly-language version all other things being equal. If you think that BASIC is fast enough, you have not sat at your computer keyboard for several hours waiting for a mailing list program sort to finish—one that would have taken 5 minutes in an assembly-language version.

SOFTWARE TIP NUMBER 6:
BUY SOFTWARE THAT CAN BE BACKED UP!

People like Trader Dick have pirated a great deal of software and deprived many companies from their just profits and software authors from their fair royalties. Because of this, some companies have gone to nonstandard disk formats that cannot be backed up. If a single disk is used repeatedly, there is a good chance at some future point it will become unreadable, due to excessive handling or simply acts of God. At that point, a manufacturer will tell you, "We will be happy to send you another copy for a nominal fee." What if the manufacturer is no longer around? There goes your beautiful data base of the last year's commodities markets.

Some smaller software companies and larger microcomputer manufacturers alike are producing diskettes that can be backed up not at all or only once or twice. If you are certain that the company you are buying the software from will be around for the next few years, and if the program on diskette can be backed up at least once, then the backup problem is not that critical. However, do not buy this type of program from a smaller, undercapitalized, garage-shop operation. The business may be well intentioned, but you are taking a gamble!

SOFTWARE TIP NUMBER 7:
BUY SOFTWARE FROM RESPONSIVE COMPANIES

For example, companies selling a completely functioning microcomputer at a price of under $100 are probably not going to be extremely responsive to their customers. One of the understandings of such a product is that the company cannot afford to give hours of software or hardware support for a hundred thousand users that call up and query them on operating procedures or construction advice.

On the other hand, if you buy an applications program or operating system for $500 or more, you should expect some answers to thorny questions or unusual problems that cannot be gleaned from the instruction manual in a reasonable amount of time.

The question is, of course, just *how much* support should be given per dollar value of software. Certainly, someone should be held accountable for bugs in the software; there should be someone that responds to legitimate bugs that users find. You will find, however, that some manufacturers and software houses have what can only be called a flagrant disregard for even knowledgeable users that call in with valid problems. Some of the smallest garage shops, however, are the most receptive to questions and problems. Choose software from responsive companies.

SOFTWARE TIP NUMBER 8:
EVALUATE SOFTWARE USING A VARIETY
OF TECHNIQUES

Even an inexpensive software package is worth extensive evaluation. The initial cost of the package is nothing compared to the time and data that you will be investing in it if you use it considerably.

Word of mouth is probably one of the best evaluation techniques. If you have a group of users or computer club in your area, check to see whether anyone has the program, ask them how they like it, and check on potential problems. If you have a system with a data communication capability, another good way of getting independent evaluations of software is to use the bulletin boards, or such services as CompuServe to question other computer users on software. (CompuServe has special interest groups that will have many members for your particular microcomputer.)

Magazine reviews are also good for evaluation. I know that manufacturers advertise in magazines. I know that advertising revenues are important. However, in spite of that, I feel that most magazines give objective reviews to software products; in fact, some of the reviews may be even a little too critical because of the nature of criticism in general.

SOFTWARE TIP NUMBER 9:
SEE THE SOFTWARE DEMONSTRATED IF POSSIBLE

Many computer stores will not only let you see an operating version of a software package, they will let you actually exercise it. Don't forget, you will be spending a great deal of time with some software applications, so it is worth your while to actually exercise and test the-package before you buy it.

There are some flaws in this approach, however. Larger software packages may be so powerful that it takes a considerable amount of time to learn how to do the most basic things with them. In this case, you probably cannot afford the time to learn a significant portion of the procedures for operating the package. Again, it may not be fair to ask the computer store to spend hours giving you a demonstration, either.

These are the tips that Rick used in successfully buying software packages for his system. Although there is no guarantee that you will wind up with a Corniche, a yacht, and a twin-engine light plane if you follow these tips, you will be at least able to use your system efficiently without having to sort through 100 different diskettes.

SOFTWARE CHECKLIST

For further consideration, here is a checklist of items to help you make the right choices on software, including additional items not covered in this chapter.

- What operating system will the software use—the standard OS for your system, or another, or all?
- What language is the program written in?
- How much disk storage does the package take? How much disk storage is left over for use of files?
- How flexible is it? Can the input and output formats be defined by the user or are they fixed?
- How much RAM memory does it take when it is loaded? What are the minimum RAM requirements for using the package? What is the minimum RAM for practical use?
- How much does the package cost?
- How much are new versions?
- Will there be enhancements to new versions?
- Will you get notification of the new version automatically?
- Is the system unconditionally guaranteed to be free of program bugs? What do you have to do to get a replacement?
- Can you back the program up using standard backup procedures for your system? If not, will it back-up itself? If so, how many backups can be made?
- Is it easy to use?
- Is it *menu-driven* and *self-prompting*?
- Is there adequate documentation?
- Is there a training course in addition to the manual?
- Is there customer support in the form of someone who can answer general questions by phone? by mail?
- Can it be modified to work with nonstandard input/ output devices? For example, can you use a serial printer in place of a standard parallel printer?
- Have there been any reviews in magazines? What did they say?
- Are there local users who could be contacted for their references?

Section

3

Applications and Procedures

How To Use Disk Files

In the last section operating systems for microcomputers were talked about and some of the physical aspects of disk drives were described. In this chapter let us assume that you were so awed by the potential of disk drive storage for your system that you purchased one or more disk drives. In a lot of cases, the cost of the disk drives is as much as the cost of the basic computer system. You now have a great deal of expensive hardware sitting there; how do you use it?

To use disk drives efficiently, you have got to learn something about *disk files*. Nothing invokes more fear in beginning computer users than such black magic incantations as *sequential files, random files,* and *variable-length records*. In this chapter you will find out how to protect yourself against spells cast by demons using these ominous words. Do you have your pentagram drawn on the floor? Step inside while I utter the following magic words . . .

DISK FREE SPACE

To begin with, look the devil in the eye and shout "Disk Free Space!" This is the amount of space that is available to hold all of your disk information. If your system has only one 5¼-inch disk drive and a large disk operating system, you may have only 50,000 bytes or so of disk free space. If you have a system with several 8-inch disk drives, you may have 500,000 bytes per disk drive. (If you have a Winchester-type disk drive on your system with 10 megabytes of storage, you are too affluent for this book. Hire your own consultant . . .)

Whatever the storage available, you must be able to store data in the space available and retrieve it rapidly. All disk drives should be able to access any data in the free space in under a few seconds, and that is the beauty of disk storage.

All disk BASIC versions and all operating systems have a built in *file-manage* capability. This is system software that handles allocation of the free space on the disk. The disk free space is segmented into disk *files* as the need arises.

WHAT IS A FILE?

What is Truth? What is Beauty? The term *file* is somewhat less abstract. Marginally. A file is any collection of meaningful data. It is anything that would normally be in a separate file cabinet section, such as a record of all the people who have purchased widgets from your company, the last ten years of your income tax returns, your accounting books (you may need two separate files for these), a mailing list, or a record of temperatures for the last 12 months.

But . . . It is also a BASIC program of 200 lines, a game program written in assembly language, and a piece of system software.

When used in conjunction with a microcomputer system, then, a file is a set of data records, a BASIC program, an assembly language or a higher-level language program (such as a Pascal program file), or a system program file. A broad division between these many file examples might be a *data file* or a *program file*.

FILE STRUCTURE

Has any of that sulfur and brimstone smoke cleared yet? No? Let me murmur the Latin phrase, "File Recordix!" Every file is subdivided into *records*. A record is analogous to a file folder within a filing cabinet section. A mail list data file, for example, would have a separate record for each name. If there were 1,000 names in the mail list file, there would be 1,000 records. An inventory program data file would have a separate record for each part number. A data file containing weather data for the past 12 months would have a separate record for each of the 365 days.

What about program files? Here, also, the file is divided into records. A BASIC program would be organized with a separate record for each line of the program. An assembly-language program might group the *machine code* of the program into blocks of 256 bytes, each block defining a record. However, unless you are investigating the structure of all disk files, you will not have to be concerned with records within program files. Just think of them as one huge file and forget about the internal subdivisions.

So far the subdivisions shown in Fig. 11-1 have been discussed. Free disk space, a number of separate files, and records within the files are the major subdivisions. Are there further subdivisions?

The next level down takes us from the filing cabinet analogy into computer jargon. Records are divided into *fields*. A field is any logical subdivision of data in a record.

In a mail list file, for example, each record might have eight fields, one for the last name, one for the first name, one for the company name, one for the street address, one for the city, one for the state, one for the zip code, and one comment field. An accounts receivable record might have a field for account number code, name, balance, 30 days overdue, 60 days overdue, 90 days overdue, over 90 days overdue, and comments. Some examples are shown in Fig. 11-2.

HOW LONG IS A RECORD?

No, this isn't a riddle, so don't give me that business about "long enough to reach the disk drive . . ." The record length is a crucial question with disk files. In a manual filing system it is possible to squeeze in some marginal notes on an account card or to add some further comments on an accounts receivable record, such

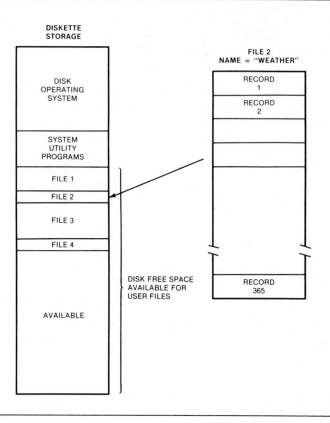

Fig. 11-1. Disk file structure.

as "suing the living daylights . . ." In a computer data file, however, you must be aware of the sizes of records and fields.

In general, a disk file may contain any number of *records*, up to the limits of the free space available on a diskette. In fact, the file may even span several diskettes with file segments on many separate diskettes although this does not make for efficient handling of files.

Records within the file, however, may be either *fixed-length* or *variable-length*. Which type to use is directly related to the speed and efficiency of data files on your computer system.

136

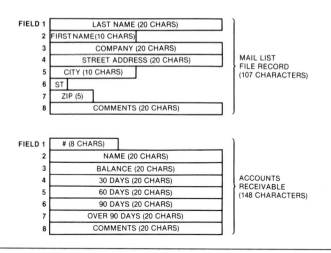

Fig. 11-2. Fields in records.

VARIABLE-LENGTH RECORDS AND SEQUENTIAL FILES

As the name implies, a *variable-length record* may be any number of bytes. Taking the case of a mail list, for example, record number 1 might be "BARDEN, BILL, 250 N.S. MEMORY LANE, COMPUTERTOWN, CA, 92692, NOTE: PARSIMONIOUS B." and record number 2 might be "GIANT COMPUTER CO., PO BOX 12, THUD, ID". The first record is 79 characters (counting spaces, which are counted as characters), and the second record is 39 characters.

With variable-length records, the disk file manage generally uses a type of file called a *sequential file*. Because the records are varying lengths, the file is written out to disk in sequence from beginning record to ending record. When the records are read in, the disk file manage program of the disk operating system reads in the next record, whether it is 1 character or 1,000 characters.

To locate the 175th record, the disk file manage must start at the beginning of the file, and read (and discard) 174 records before it finally finds and transmits the 175th record to your BASIC (or other language) program. In other words, the data in this file is read and written *sequentially*, from beginning to end. As the records are variable length, the disk file manage does not know where to look to find the "nth" record.

Sequential files are fine for data that normally would be processed from beginning to end. However, for data that must be processed at *random*, they are not very efficient. Imagine a clerk answering a phone call from Anthony Zerbopopodopolous— "Just a moment, sir. Let me get your file. Let's see, Aardvark, Albert; Andrews, Robert; Anders, John . . . . . . Zamski, Ed; Zerbopopodopolous, Anthony. Got it! Sir? . . . Sir? Are you there?"

The same situation occurs in finding or merging data in sequential files. To overcome this costly overhead in locating a random record, a *random file* can be used on some systems. (Random files are sometimes called *indexed* files.)

FIXED-LENGTH RECORDS AND RANDOM FILES

In a random file, each record is a *fixed length*. Taking the mail list file as an example, suppose that each record is 100 characters long. To locate the 175th record, then, we would simply have to find the 17,500th character in the file. The disk file manage would know that the 175th record would occupy characters from 17,500 through 17,599 in the file, and it could find the record very easily by going directly to the spot in the disk file where the record started.

Of course, in microcomputers as well as other things, one never gets something for nothing. The price we have to pay for rapid access in a fixed-length record, random file is: (1) Waste of space, (2) Complexity.

Because the records are fixed-length, we must allow for the largest record in the file, or we must live with some data being shortened. It might be necessary to limit the last name to 16 characters, for example, alienating Anthony when he gets his brochure on new computer systems addressed to A. Zerbopopodopolo!

Since many records will not use up all of the space allocated per record, this unused space is wasted, and increases the file size over a sequential file.

Furthermore, random files are somewhat harder to set up than sequential files. To find data within a record, the *fields* for the record must be defined by BASIC (or other) statements, and this complicates the programming. In addition, some arithmetic may have to be done to locate the record number within the file.

Another complexity about random files is that more attention must be paid to the physical characteristics of the disk drive itself and the format of the diskettes used in the drive. Random files work best in multiples of *sector lengths.* As discussed previously, a disk sector is typically 256 *bytes* (roughly corresponding to 256 characters), and ideal records for this sector size would be multiples or submultiples of 256, such as 64-byte records, 128-byte records, 256-byte records, and so forth.

ISAM, YOUSAM, WEALLSAM FOR DISK FILES

Well, do you feel that you've overcome your fear of the black magic disk file buzzwords? Better get out your garlic strands, because we've got another demon to fight. "ISAM!" shouted the devil, as he advanced towards the microcomputer user . . .

ISAM stands for Indexed Sequential Access Method. It is an old file manage technique of allocating space on disk. (By old, I mean 20 years or so.) ISAM is touted as a separate package to be used in conjunction with existing disk operating systems.

ISAM is a method of combining the features of both sequential-access files and random-access files. Basically, space is left at significant points throughout the files so that no records can be added without reshuffling the entire file. The overall effect is to make file management more efficient at the expense of program complexity.

Is ISAM worth the cost and learning time? If your system does a great deal of file operation, then it may be worth your while to consider an ISAM software package for your system. If you simply read in a data file in the morning and write it out at night, then it probably is not worth considering.

Small computer software is becoming more and more sophisticated and other file manage packages in addition to ISAM will be offered. As with any software, buy from a reputable company that will give you solid support. Be prepared to invest some time in understanding the operation of the package, and it may prove to be a valuable adjunct to your system operation.

ASCII AND OTHER FILES

Just a few more explanations, and we'll complete the exorcism of those disk file fears . . .

Up to this point we have been primarily considering data files that have *character* data in them—readable data such as alphabetic, numeric, and special characters (# and ★). Files made up completely of this type of character data are called *ASCII* files.

ASCII files are nice because they are computer independent. You can, for example, take a TRS-80 Model III ASCII data file from your microcomputer system, send it over the phone lines by means of a communication interface to an IBM Personal Computer, and have the IBM system process the file without any problem. You could not, however, take a TRS-80 Model III BASIC program file, perform the same transfer, and have the IBM system successfully execute the program even though the BASIC statements might be compatible.

NonASCII files, such as BASIC program files, assembly-language program files, word-processing files, and others, compress data into shorter form. The result is a much shorter file than would occur if the data was in ASCII codes. If your system can generate both BASIC program files and BASIC program files in ASCII, write the same program in ASCII and nonASCII mode. You will find the nonASCII version much shorter.

The same techniques can be used with your data files by using random files and, in some cases, sequential files. An ASCII string of the numeric value 12345, for example, takes up 5 bytes of disk space or RAM (random-access memory) in ASCII form. Properly coded in *binary* format, the same value will only occupy 2 bytes! A good example would be our over-exampled mail list data file. The new 9-digit zip codes could be compressed from 9 bytes of disk or memory storage to 4 bytes by using binary data. Again, this would be at the expense of program complexity and time spent in learning the techniques.

DISK FILE CONSIDERATIONS

Now that you have successfully cleared some of the hellish smoke from disk files, let us talk about some of the pragmatic considerations.

If you are contemplating a microcomputer system purchase, it is very important to get a system that efficiently handles disk files. In essence, this is directly related to the efficiency of the operating system that comes with the system as previously discussed.

If you have some BASIC programming experience or you have a friend who is knowledgeable in BASIC, do not hesitate to run some benchmark programs to test the computer systems.

A short BASIC program of 15 lines or so can be run on a number of systems while you time the total elapsed time with a stopwatch. Of course, you may be criticized by the salesman while you do, but tell him to go back to the carnival con game! An example of a program that was used to compare an IBM Personal Computer system with a Radio Shack TRS-80 Model III is shown in Fig. 11-3.

Look into the amount of free storage available on the system diskettes. The more storage, of course, the more powerful the system will be in storing your data files.

Look at the types of files allowed. Are sequential files and random files allowed? Is it difficult to set up random files? Are there commands in the BASIC language that will allow you to define fields in random files and to process them? Are there any ISAM or other file management schemes that can be used with the operating system?

```
100   REM BENCHMARK FOR FILE OPERATIONS
110   CLEAR 10000
120   FOR I = 100 TO 1000 STEP 100
130   CLS
140   A$ = STRING$(80,"*")
150   OPEN "O",1,"TEST:1"
160   LPRINT"START TIME FOR ";I;"RECORDS";TIME$
170   FOR J = 1 TO I
180   PRINT #1,A$: PRINT J
190   NEXT J
200   LPRINT "END TIME FOR";I;"RECORDS";TIME$
210   CLOSE 1
220   KILL "TEST:1"
230   NEXT I
240   PRINT "END"
```

Fig. 11-3. Benchmark test program.

What about the operating system? Does it conveniently allow you to list the files on disk, to delete and rename them?

Proper use of disk files is one of the most important considerations in increasing the usability, speed, and efficiency of your BASIC programs. Look upon this discussion as an introduction to the subject, and try to gain practical experience and knowledge by using all of the capabilities on your system. It may require some effort, but it will be an excellent investment. You may still beat the devil at the old disk file game!

Never Lose Data on Your Disk Again!

Once upon a midnight dreary, as I pondered, weak and weary, over many a volume of forgotten code, there came a knocking, gentle knocking, at my disk drive door.

There I was, working the prime hours that programmers get at the end of the product development cycle. We were almost ready to ship the product, a large-scale computerized tester, and the programmers were working three shifts to make the final changes to the software for the tester.

The knocking at the disk drive door came from a crashed disk, a condition in larger disk drives where the heads come crashing down on the surface of the disk. All of my programs were on that disk! What to do, what to do . . .

Fortunately, I had made backups of the disk. I would only lose what I had done over the past 4 hours, and I could recover most of that by doing about an hour of work in editing the programs. I loaded the backup disk that I had made the previous day and "rebooted" the system.

Quoth the system, "NEVERMORE." To my horror, I found that this disk would not load—it appeared to be damaged! No more backups on disk—I'd have to go to the punched cards. And that was complicated by the fact that our nervous computer operator had dropped most of the punched cards the prior day! It looked like another fun evening shuffling punched cards, reassembling the programs, verifying that everything was in order, and then creating a new disk cartridge.

An unusual situation? Yes. Recoverable? Yes, with 12 hours of work. But things have changed since those dark days when computer systems were unreliable, haven't they? Absolutely not! In this chapter let us discuss some of the failures that can occur in your computer system and what you can do to make your system "fail-safe."

CODERS IN THE HANDS OF AN ANGRY GOD

Let us discuss the least common type of failure first—what lawyers call *force majeure*—World War III, tornados, hurricanes, tidal waves, and, way down on the bottom of the list, such things as power failures or turning off the computer system with diskettes still in the drive.

When power fails in any electronic system, the circuits do not work in orderly fashion. In that fraction of a second while the power goes from "full on" to zero, tens of thousands of microprocessor instructions might be executed. Some of those instructions might be ones that would garble data on the disk although this is not too likely.

A far greater danger is that current will travel through the disk drive recording head and write "garbage" to a portion of the diskette in the disk drive or drives. This has happened to me more than once and will probably happen again.

What about the case of an unexpected power down, such as a lightning strike during computer operation or an unreliable power company? (Or through operator error—one of my computers has an expansion disk drive chassis with a power switch located exactly at my knee level!) Is there any way to recover lost files on the disk?

The best way, of course, is by throwing away the disk in question and putting in a backup disk. If you do not have a backup, however, you may be able to recover some of the data, depending upon what type it is.

If the data is a data file of information, you may be able to read in part of the data by altering your BASIC or other program slightly to read in as much data as possible and then to write it out as a good file. This would mean bypassing parts of the program that would normally detect error conditions.

Possibly your programs and data files on the disk are intact, but the operating system software is partially destroyed. In this case, you may be able to use a second disk drive to copy your intact programs or data files from the bad disk to a new disk.

If the data on the zapped disk is very important and irreplaceable, there are some utility programs for the more popular computer systems that allow you to bypass the operating system file manage and go directly to the physical disk sectors to retrieve the data. This may, however, require intimate knowledge of how the operating system structures its disk directories and files, information generally poorly documented.

One of the failings of most software provided for microcomputers is that it incorporates the tough-luck syndrome. When a BASIC program has other data read in from disk, the software will proceed normally if all the data is successfully read in. If one error occurs, however, the software will figuratively throw up its hands and shout "Tough Luck!" with an error message. This occurs even though only one bit in the program or data is bad! In most cases this is fine, as many programs will operate improperly if even a single bit is bad. In other cases, such as word-processing files, it would be more convenient to provide a warning message and leave it up to the user to reconstruct the data or to determine how much is bad. The error routines are normally buried within the internals of the operating system, and it takes a very astute programmer to bypass the normal "Tough Luck!" action.

"BURNING-IN" CAN AVOID LATER SLOW BURN

Hardware failures are the most common cause of disk problems. Hardware failures are caused by the same things that cause any complicated piece of machinery to fail—many parts connected together to make up a device. Newer microcomputers have fewer and fewer parts, fewer and fewer semiconductor chips. In general, even though the complexity of the semiconductor chips is very great—tens of thousands of equivalent transistors on a single chip—fewer chips means fewer failures.

Even the most stringent testing, however, may fail to detect marginal chips that will eventually fail. Often, chip failure is in the early hours of operation—the so-called "infant mortality." Some manufacturers will "burn in" microcomputers for many hours to weed out these initial failures.

Disk drives are not only electronic components in a computer system—they are electromechanical devices. Electromechanical devices are even more prone to failures than purely electrical devices.

Can anything be done about disk hardware failures, other than uttering a "Doggone disk drive!" when the failure occurs?

First of all, burn in the system for several days when you get it. Admittedly, this calls for some caution, as microcomputers are electrical devices and can cause fires. Make a "sniff test" around the equipment—things may smell warm, but there should be no unpleasant odors, such as the distinctive odor of "component flambe."

In addition, touch the exposed parts of the system. You should, in general, be able to leave your finger on any metal parts. If you cannot, the microcomputer or peripheral device may be improperly heat sunk. A case that comes to mind is a popular microcomputer manufacturer that had disk drives with rear-mounted power supplies that in many cases were improperly assembled for heat dissipation.

Now here is where the fail-safe aspect comes in for disk hardware failures. Obtain and run *diagnostic programs*. Diagnostic programs are special programs that test and exercise the proper operation of the microprocessor, memory, printer, disk drives, and other system components. In some cases these are provided by the manufacturer, but in many cases they are not.

A comprehensive disk diagnostic program will test the functions of the disk, and then exercise the disk by repeated operations. A disk drive diagnostic will write out certain data patterns to the disk, including a worst case and some random data.

Many times a diagnostic will reveal marginal disk problems that will later appear as hard failures—a failing sector on disk, or frequent disk I/O errors.

Run the diagnostic at regular intervals, say, every Monday. If errors do occur on the disk diagnostic, have the system repaired before hard errors occur and destroy valuable data.

Another tip—keep a *system maintenance log*. This is a notebook in which you should list any disk or system malfunction, imagined or not. This will provide a record of failure patterns that will prove useful.

SOFTWARE NEVER FAILS
ONCE IT IS CHECKED OUT

A computer engineer I know once told me, "You've got it lucky. Once you've got the software designed and debugged, it runs forever!" Sure. Little did he know about the disgruntled programmer who, shortly before his termination was effective, built in a bug that read the date of each day and destroyed every installation of the manufacturer's disk operating system on his birthday!

Bugs do not have to be built in; they are there. And sometimes blatantly, too. All microcomputer manufacturers are aware of bugs in released software, some minor, some major. The better manufacturers "'fess up" and publish the bugs with corrections. The worst ones will not admit there are bugs or act arrogant when they are pointed out!

In many cases, you must be aware of these bugs and live with them. Disk file manage is complicated. Furthermore, many programmers regard writing software drivers that communicate with complicated peripherals as a black art. Because of these reasons, software that handles disk operations is prone to bugs.

A typical bug found in early manufacturer's software (since corrected) that you may have to put up with: BASIC interpreter destroys the disk when a disk full condition exists!

The best way to make all your software fail-safe is to obtain it from a reliable source. Before purchase, if possible, read reviews of the software; reviewers will tell you what outstanding bugs there are, if any. Word of mouth in software is an excellent way to choose software as it is in other areas.

Finally, if you are running a program that replaces an existing manual system, such as order entry, run the software in parallel with your existing system until you are confident that the software operates properly. Do not just enter your precious business or personal data into that "star-quality" applications program. It may turn out to be a black hole, and you may never see the light of your orders again. Be paranoid.

WHEN EQUIPMENT AND SOFTWARE
IMPROVE WITH AGE

Another source of disk problems is operator error. Have you noticed when using a new piece of equipment or software how the number of errors diminish after several weeks? Usually the equipment or software runs perfectly after that period. I start by being very suspicious of the new product and nod my head sagely while muttering something about "program bugs" as the program destroys my disks or generally reduces my data to piles of tangled yarn.

There is no question that improper operating procedures can cause irreparable damage to disk files. How can operator error be avoided?

First, study the operating procedures for the programs you will be using. In all fairness, these programs should be "idiot-proof"—you should never be able to destroy the program itself or the disk files while running the program. The program should detect invalid keyboard responses, provide help by good menus, and offer corrective message action on errors. In actual practice, there are some programs that may destroy themselves and disk files by improper responses. The only solution is to make certain that you operate the program correctly.

Secondly, be familiar with your system components—the microcomputer, peripheral devices, and other hardware. Here again, there should be virtually nothing you can do to harm the equipment by programming or operation. In practice, however, you can abuse the system components, especially electromechanical devices such as disk drives. It would not be recommended procedure, for example, to run certain repetitive tests on a disk diagnostic for hours; excessive heat might damage disk components.

Thirdly, develop good operating practices. The most important of these is backup, and that leads us to the thrust of this chapter.

THE BACKUP HIERARCHY

The basic premise in backup is that your computer system will monitor your biorythms, and then knock you down at your most susceptible point. It will then kick you while you're down. You can protect yourself with the ancient martial art of backup.

Like many things, there is a "risk-benefit" factor in backups. You do not want to spend 20% of your time making backups; on the other hand you do not want to run an inventory program for three months without duplicating some of the data. Backup is a form of insurance.

It is not unreasonable to assume that your computer system will fail twice a year. Base your backup actions on this approximate figure. A backup of a 5¼-inch floppy diskette will take less than three minutes on most systems with a single disk operating system command. If you make a backup once every 8-hour day, less than 1% of your time will be spent in this form of insurance, making it one of the more attractive insurance bargains around (in spite of the protests of my agent!).

The typical backup hierarchy for data files is shown in Fig. 12-1. You are probably generating reports with your applications program, and these reports are probably run on a daily or periodic basis. Since these reports are usually saved, they form the bulwarks of your backup defense. Ideally, an operator should be able to reconstruct all input data from keying in the information on these reports if you lose *all* your disks.

If information is missing on these reports, you might want to consider adding additional reports or reformatting the reports so that the data can be reconstructed in this manner.

Depending upon your application, you may merge data from a *transaction file* to create a new *master file,* or you may simply be keying in data on an irregular basis. In any event, you will probably create a new master file periodically. This new master should replace the old master. The new master can replace a *third generation* diskette.

Needless to say, all diskettes should include the date on which the transactions were made.

The number of diskettes used depends upon the importance of the data, the (current) reliability of your system, and the frequency of your updates. If your system has exhibited symptoms of malaise (such as recoverable disk errors) make more backups than you normally do; if it has been running fine for months, a three-disk backup scheme might be fine.

Small diskettes can be purchased in bulk for about $2.50 per diskette; eight-inch diskettes can be purchased for about $4.50 per diskette. If you would like to keep a year of transactions, you may want to spend a $650 premium for a year of backups, or you may want to keep a smaller amount. Again, it is how important the data is to you.

The backups of programs shown in Fig. 12-2 are handled in a similar fashion. If you are developing a program, keep three diskettes, one with the current version of the program, one with the last version, and one with the version prior to the last version. Again, expand the number of diskettes if program modifications are being frequently done.

Each program version should be labeled *in the program* with a *version/revision number.* The *version number* represents the

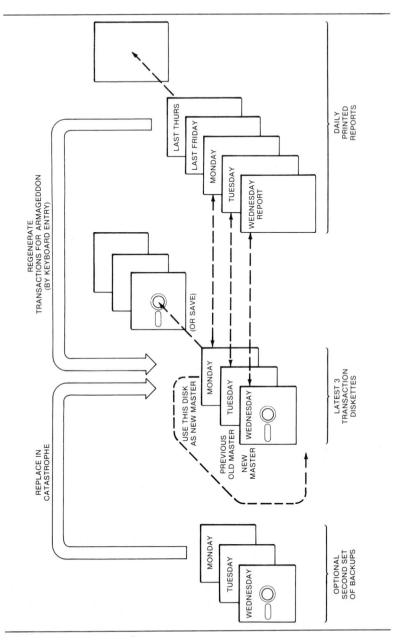

Fig. 12-1. Backup hierarchy for data files.

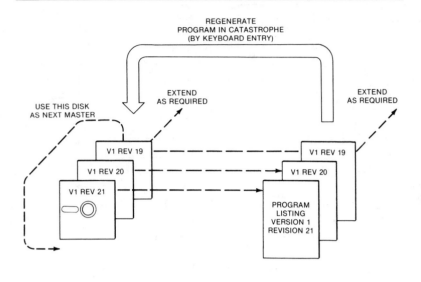

Fig. 12-2. Backup hierarchy for program files.

version of the program being developed. The *revision number* is a consecutive number of the program revision.

Each backup of the program on disk should have a clearly labeled listing of the program. More than one programmer has tried to update and edit an old version of a program.

COPYRIGHT IS NOT THE RIGHT TO COPY

Some programs from manufacturers are on diskettes that cannot be backed up. It takes neophyte microcomputer users about 50 milliseconds to realize that they might be able to get a disk full of $200 programs from a friend, rather than spending the equivalent amount for programs from the software developer. Programs that cannot be backed up by standard backup procedures eliminate loss of sales by illegal copies.

Unfortunately, many people would like several backups of important software without having to rely on additional (albeit low cost) copies from the developer. This is an extremely controversial topic, so let us just try to present a few facts:

- There are products commonly available for low cost (less than $50) that will copy virtually any disk.
- There are programmers who have the expertise to use these products or their own programs to copy any disk.
- Almost every microcomputer user (save thee and me) has copied some program without buying it; many users have thousands of dollars worth of software that they have never paid for.
- Copying has indeed prevented many companies from developing new products and destroyed other software developers.
- No one wants a single copy of an important applications program.
- It is true—to some problems there are no solutions.

NEVER LOSE DATA ON YOUR DISK AGAIN!

No, unlike the car polishing ad, I cannot guarantee that you will never have disk problems. They will be there, if only in the form of acts of God. However, if you *do* perform periodic backups, and you *do* follow some of the suggestions above in regard to hardware and software disk failures, you will be providing inexpensive insurance for that day when you hear the knocking on your disk drive door and the operating system intones "NEVERMORE . . ."

Teaching Your Computer To Use the Phone — Data Communications

Arthur C. Clarke once wrote a science-fiction story about the telephone system. In his story, the interconnections of a world-wide telephone system became a huge brain that takes over the world. His premise was that the number of telephone interconnections surpassed the number of neurons in the human brain. If this prophecy ever comes to pass, *data communications* will make it easy for Ma Bell (and her counterpart, Ivan Bell) to accomplish world-wide control of traffic flow, industrial processes, and personal computers.

In this chapter you will become prepared for the time when you become a slave to your personal computer via data communications. (Maybe your spouse already holds this view!) Let us investigate data communications—what it is, how computers are hooked up to such services as The Source and CompuServe and each other, and what you need to use it.

COMPUTER DATA: BINARY DECISIVENESS

Data communications is really just a transfer of data over long distances and over existing facilities. To understand data communications we have to understand a little bit about data transfer in computers and a little bit about data itself.

Data in computers is any organized set of numbers representing computer instructions, text, or user data files. All data in personal and other computers, of course, is broken down into binary values—ones and zeroes. This includes everything from microprocessor signals representing *clock* pulses of the microcomputer system occurring millions of times per second to transfers of bytes between the microprocessor and memory and to transfers of text characters between the microprocessor and your system line printer.

Why binary? Why ones and zeroes? The main reason is that a computer can never be indecisive. It must know that a signal is either off or on, a one or a zero. If a computer were constructed of components that indicated 10 states, such as 0 volts, 1 volt, 2 volts, up to 9 volts, the circuits would be hard to maintain and subject to "aging" and "creep" of signals—8 volts might become 8.5 volts, and 9 volts might become 8.5 volts, and there it is—thermonuclear war or, at least, a malfunction in your Alien Invaders game.

The next larger grouping of data, as everyone who has been in microcomputers more than 50 milliseconds knows, is a *byte* or collection of 8 bits. Why are things organized in bytes? Why not in 16 bits or 32 bits? The main reason is that manufacturers "would if they could." Most of our microcomputers are 8-bit microprocessors because of physical limitations on the microprocessor chip—number of circuits that can be packed on the chip and number of output pins. Another reason is that text data can be nicely represented in 8 bits. Eight bits can hold 256 "permutations" of things—numbers from decimal 0 through decimal 255, and this is more than enough to represent all keyboard characters.

DATA PATHS: 8 BITS AND SERIAL

Data paths in computers are organized into multiples of 8-bit bytes. There are 8 data signal lines from microprocessor to memory and from microprocessor to input/output devices such printers.

Now suppose that we want to connect a remote terminal, such as a keyboard and display, to a computer located some distance away. The advantages of this are obvious. We can have an inexpensive keyboard and display, a so-called *video display terminal* or VDT, as a remote input to a more expensive computer system. Maybe we can have dozens of VDTs all connected to a central computer system. How do we do it?

One way would be to route wires from computer to VDTs. Eight sets of wires for data plus some additional wires for signal lines could be routed to every VDT.

This is a possible solution, but it has several problems. First of all, copper wires cost money. If the runs are several feet, well and good. If the runs are miles, though, costs can mount rapidly. Secondly, there are electrical limitations on rapidly changing signals; the lines tend to be noisy and erratic. Thirdly, and this is the real key, how do you route wires across public streets, over mountain ranges, and through swamps?

The answer is to use existing facilities. What better facility than telephone lines, which are already strung over every square foot of terrain in the world, with the possible exception of Milwaukee? (There are other alternatives—what about radio or television? However, these are only one direction—from the sponsor to the home.)

Telephone lines, however, come in pairs. They do not easily allow 8 bits of data to be passed in parallel. I say easily because there are various schemes to send larger chunks of data. Touch-Tone dialing relies on 12 different tones. Some variation of this could possibly be used to send data in 3- or 4-bit groups. However, telephone lines, especially those that are not conditioned for data communications uses, tend to be noisy. It seems, at best, 1 bit of data can reliably be sent over telephone lines.

How can 8 bits of data representing text or other information be converted to a form that can be sent over phone lines? The data is serialized to a one bit at a time form.

SERIALIZATION

Eight-bit quantities are converted to serial form by taking the individual bits and arranging them in order. One bit is sent out at a time starting with the least significant bit. An example is shown in Fig. 13-1.

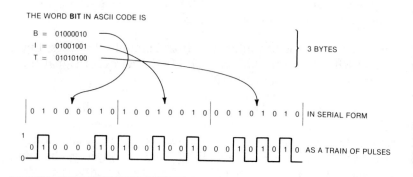

Fig. 13-1. Serialization of data.

There is a problem with this scheme, however. We can now hook up a VDT with a computer and run two wires or use the existing telephone wires. But how do we synchronize the data? How does the VDT know when data is coming in from the computer and vice versa?

The solution here is to keep the line in a known condition—either a 1 or a 0 when no data is being transmitted. The convention chosen is to keep the line in a 1 state. Whenever data is transmitted, the line is brought to a 0 state, for a short time, and then the 8 bits of data are transmitted, as shown in Fig. 13-2.

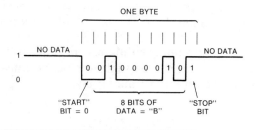

Fig. 13-2. Standard serial data format.

Bringing the line to a 0 state signals the receiving device that data is coming in, and it can prepare to receive it.

At the end of the 8 bits of data, the line is put back into a non-transmitting mode by returning it to a 1 state. The bit used to start the data transmission is, appropriately enough, called the *start bit* (a 0). The bit used to end the data transmission is called the *stop* bit (a 1). There are 8 data bits in between.

There is one obvious problem with this scheme. The receiving device can detect the start bit and look for the data easily enough. But how fast does the data come in? The 10 bits (start, 8 bits of data, and stop) must be sent at precise intervals so that the receiving device knows when to look for the next bit, as shown in Fig. 13-3.

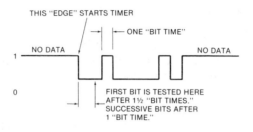

Fig. 13-3. Synchronization of data.

This interval time is measured by *baud rate,* a bit of jargonese for the number of bits per second. If we have 10 bits in our serial scheme, then a *baud rate* of 300 translates to 300/10 or 30 bytes of data per second. There is a set of standard baud rates used on microcomputer and other computer systems that includes 110, 300, 600, 1200, 2400, 4800, and 9600 baud and corresponds to 10, 30, 60, 120, 240, 480, and 960 bytes per second.

THE RS-232C STANDARD

The scheme described above is called *RS-232C.* RS-232C, known by its intimates as *RS-232* or *serial,* is a standard way of transmitting data on microcomputer systems. You probably have an

RS-232C port on your computer or can get one as an inexpensive option. When you have an RS-232C port, you have all you need to hook up your computer upstairs with the one downstairs, or your computer with a VDT downstairs, or your computer with a friend's across the street. (You do need an RS-232C program, but they are readily available at modest cost.) Simply string two wires, and connect the equipment. . . .

ENTER MA BELL

Oh, oh . . . You're right, we've forgotten about the telephone lines. We can now easily interface via two wires, providing we can control those two wires and the signals that go across them. However, this is not the case for communication thousands of miles away.

To go over telephone lines we need some way of changing the serial data into *telephone-type signals*. Telephone-type signals are rigidly defined by Ma Bell. Only certain frequencies are permitted, believe it or not. High frequencies are filtered out and certain frequencies are dedicated to Touch-Tone keys and other functions.

The standard way of converting serial data into telephone-type signals is by a *modem*. Modem stands for modulator/demodulator, another bit of jargon for converting a 0 into one audio tone, a 1 into another audio tone and vice versa. Computer modems simply take the 0 and 1 bits of the serial data and convert them (by the modulator) into two different tones. The tones are transmitted over telephone lines and reconverted to ones and zeroes by the *demodulator* part of the modem on the other end, as shown in Fig. 13-4.

MODEMS AND COUPLERS

There are two distinct types of modems. One type of modem attaches directly to the phone line and from there is *hardwired* to your RS-232C port. This is normally called a modem. The second type of device is really an *acoustic coupler*, but is also sometimes referred to as a modem. In the coupler, the headset of the phone

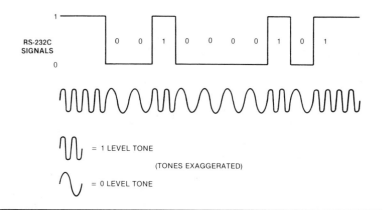

Fig. 13-4. RS-232C to modem conversion.

is laid in two rubber cups that contain a miniature loudspeaker and microphone. There is no direct electrical connection to the phone line.

The direct-connect modem is more accurate because no extraneous noise is introduced. On the other hand, you cannot pick up the direct-connect modem and hear what is going on at the other end, a desirable feature at times. Your best bet is probably a direct-connect modem hooked in parallel to a standard telephone.

Both types of modems are certified by the FCC and can be connected to your existing phone line. You should be able to do this easily simply by plugging in a jack or at worst after a trip to your local Radio Shack store.

One word of caution here. Now I'm an ATT stockholder and appreciative of the way they wired this great country of ours. However. . . . You are legally entitled to connect a certified modem to your phone line, and there should be absolutely no electrical problems of any type in doing so, nor do you have to have a business line!

In fact, the modem is a simple and inexpensive piece of hardware. Most of the complexity is in the RS-232C circuitry described previously. Modems for microcomputer use range from about $175 to $400 or so.

MICROCOMPUTER NETWORKING

Given a microcomputer with an RS-232C port, a modem, and some software, you have all you need to communicate with other remote terminals, other microcomputers, large-scale computer systems, or other communications networks.

You should note at this point that we are talking about common microcomputer communication and not large-scale computers, which may use *synchronous* data communication in another type of format, telephone lines that are specially conditioned by the phone company for computer use or specially installed telephone lines.

Most of this communication is transfer of text data—alphabetic, numeric, and special characters (#, %, etc.). This data is coded in ASCII format in almost all computer systems. ASCII uses a 7-bit code, and the eighth data bit is often used for a *parity* bit. No, farmers, it's not what you think. The eighth parity bit is a *check bit* that reflects the number of ones and zeroes in each transmitted piece of data.

Although ASCII transmission is most common, there is no reason that we cannot transmit anything that can be coded in 8-bit chunks of data, and some systems do this to transmit graphics, programs, and other data.

Modems used for microcomputers are generally 300 baud, limiting the data transfer rates to about 30 characters per second. This is due to the frequency limitations of normal telephone lines. Some modems allow up to 1,200 baud (120 characters per second) over normal telephone lines although these are in the minority at present.

CURRENT NETWORK ACTIVITY

Currently there are roughly three types of data communication networks, bulletin board systems, specialized bulletin board systems, and data communications services such as The Source and CompuServe. In addition, there are a number of experimental services being offered by banks and other institutions; in some cases even the computer is provided!

Bulletin boards are numerous and they are free. You can buy a modem that will automatically answer your phone, and these can be used (with some fairly complicated software) to implement your own bulletin board. Callers dial in and read or leave messages. It is like a central bulletin board in a market where people leave signs of all types—items they want to sell, to buy, and the like. There are even people who continue a dialog with one another spread over days on every subject from chess to poetry. And yes, there are morons who try to enter obscenities and vitriolic statements about politics, religion and computer magazine columnists.

Specialized bulletin board systems are a subset of the first type. They may be geared to specific computers like the Apple or TRS-80. They may also be geared to special interests. There is at least one system that caters to sexually related topics by means of passwords.

The third type of system is the service network such as The Source, CompuServe, or Dow-Jones. For a fee, they provide a local telephone number and a password for system access. You pay for the amount of time that you use the system and not for long distance charges. Services such as wire-service news, stock reports, weather, and user-group information are offered.

Is the latter type of service cost-effective? One of the criticisms of such services is that they are prone to over-loading. At any time they may be servicing dozens of people, and there may be inordinately long delays between the time you ask for data and the time it finally appears on your screen.

Also, 30 characters per second (or 15 characters per second in certain modes) is not a terribly high communication rate for a microcomputer that can process data at thousands of characters per second. Contrast the typical 100 words per minute average of data communications (with responses and waits) against reading your local newspaper at 400 or more words per minute. And you can read your newspaper in "random-access" mode, skipping over data you do not want and scanning forward and backwards. As of this moment I would not want my newspaper delivered by computer every day . . .

IS DATA COMMUNICATION FOR YOU?

Why not? It is inexpensive enough, probably constituting about 10% of the total cost of your system or less. Chances are that you will find services that appeal to you on the bulletin boards or service systems. Also, don't forget that you can communicate with other microcomputer users who have any model microcomputer over the standardized RS-232C port. You might even be interested in starting your own bulletin board. In spite of my snide remarks about data rates, the potential is there for automatic retrieval of information and interface to a variety of services.

One word of advice, though. If you are hooked up to a data communication network and the lights go off in your house, the television station disappears, and the video display ominously states "OK SMART GUY—I'M TAKING CONTROL NOW . . .," try to power down as quickly as possible. If you can . . .

Chapter

14

More on Data Communications — Making Your Computer Even Smarter

There was a time, back before the days of small computers, that all terminals were "dumb" terminals. As a matter of fact, about four generations ago all terminals were strictly electromechanical devices, consisting of hundreds of levers, cams, and rotating shafts. Teletype Corporation teletypewriters and similar units had all they could do to simply receive and transmit signals over *serial* data links and convert data into printable English characters.

Digital computers changed all of that. First came the "dumb" terminals, the *glass teletypewriters* that replaced such venerable older terminals as the Teletype Corporation KSR-33. The old terminals consisted of a keyboard for input (if you were lucky) and a display of ASCII character data. They were used for digital computer console devices for slow-speed data entry and display.

With the advent of microprocessors, terminals started to get smarter. Why not buffer the keyboard input and store a line of text before sending it out to the computer in one continuous burst? And why not allow editing an entire screen full of text? All that had to be done was to incorporate an 8080 or similar microprocessor in the terminal. The terminal could be made as intelligent as the manufacturer wished.

Finally, microcomputers reared their glamorous heads. Microcomputers are the ultimate terminals. They are not only extremely smart, with fourth-generation microprocessors, but they have scads of RAM memory for temporary storage and even disk drives for permanent storage! But are they terminals or the main computer itself? In this chapter let us discuss intelligent terminal software—the element that makes microcomputers the ultimate terminal. Also, you will get a look at some intelligent hardware—communications modems that are precocious offspring of the microcomputer era and can perform all kinds of tricks. In addition, let us cover the philosophical questions, such as "What is a terminal?" and "What is a computer?" along with such questions as "What is Truth?" and "What is Beauty?"

DATA COMMUNICATIONS

In the last chapter we discussed data communications from the standpoint of hardware. Let us refresh your memory with a recap of the subject before continuing on to intelligent terminal programs and modems.

Almost all small computer data communication is handled by the scheme shown in Fig. 14-1. Transmission *from* the computer to another device goes like this: The small computer has a *serial port*, also called an *RS-232C* or *RS-232* port. Data goes from this port in serial (bit stream) fashion into a modem, or modulator/demodulator. The modem converts the high-speed pulses from the RS-232C port into audio frequencies, which are then transmitted over local or long distance phone lines.

At the other end of the phone line, a modem converts the audio tones into high-speed pulses, which are then input to the RS-232C port of the receiving computer or terminal. The receiving device converts the data into displayable or printable characters.

Transmission *to* the small computer works exactly in reverse. The modem on either end is *bidirectional* and either converts and transmits audio tones, or receives audio tones and converts them into RS-232C signals.

In some cases, the modem is actually an acoustic coupler, a modem with rubber cups into which the telephone receiver is

166

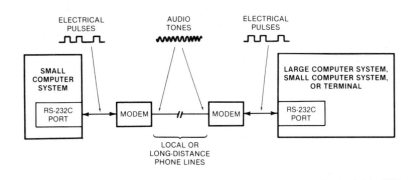

Fig. 14-1. Small computer data communication.

placed. In newer models, the modem has no acoustic input or output and connects directly to the RS-232C port.

PHILOSOPHICAL QUESTION I: WHICH IS THE TERMINAL AND WHICH IS THE COMPUTER?

It doesn't matter. There is an *originate* device and an *answer* device. The originating device is the device that "dials up" the answering device and the answering device, well . . . answers. The originate device uses one set of audio tones, while the answering device uses a second, nonconflicting set of audio tones. Data can pass both directions, even simultaneously (*full duplex*) in some cases.

Two operators can sit at two "dumb" terminals (without computer control of any kind) and communicate with one another. Operator 1 types and text appears on terminal 2. Operator 2 types and text appears on terminal 1. The two devices may be any combination of terminals, small computers, and huge computing systems, as long as all devices are equipped with RS-232C ports that supply standardized signals.

In one common use, a small computer such as an Apple or TRS-80 will be connected via phone lines to the huge computer in a communications net such as The Source or CompuServe. In another usage, a small computer may be connected to a local bulletin-board system that uses a small computer for short messages. In a third application, two users with the same computer model may be swapping programs. (Two users with different computers probably wouldn't be swapping programs only because of incompatibilities in BASIC or architecture of their machines.)

USING A SMALL COMPUTER AS A "DUMB" TERMINAL

Early software for small computers consisted mainly of RS-232C *drivers*. These drivers consisted of assembly-language code that performed two main functions: Data was received from the RS-232C port a character at a time and displayed on the screen. Keyboard text was sent out to the RS-232C port. In essence, these programs simply made the small computers glass teletypewriters.

The normal operational sequence for such a program is to manually dial up the bulletin board or network, wait for the *carrier*, a recognizable high-pitched tone, put the telephone headset in the coupler, and then wait for the *prompting* messages to be displayed on the screen as it is received from the network. After displaying *prompts* the network waits for your response, which might be your name, message, menu selection, or other data. This dialog continues until you have completed your communication.

It does not take too many hours of operation with such dumb software before the user wants something better. What about hard copy? Displays are fine, but permanent records are sometimes required. How about disk files to save programs or text? What about those systems that use nonstandard characters that cannot be generated from the keyboard of my microcomputer.

"SMART" TERMINAL PROGRAM FEATURES

In the next section a representative "smart" terminal program is described. It will list some of the features you might look for in a more practical terminal program that will make your computer unleash its processing power.

Setting the RS-232C Parameters

Almost every terminal program should have this. It allows the user to set the RS-232C interface to different communications speeds (usually 110 to 300 *baud,* or roughly 10 to 30 characters per second), word lengths, *start* and *stop* bits, and *parity.* Normal data characters are in ASCII format, a 7-bit code, and with one leading start bit and two trailing stop bits. Some networks allow eight bit codes for computer graphics; conventions for parity are not standard among the networks. There should be some means of setting various combinations of RS-232C parameters by entering a simple keyboard command.

Translation of Characters

Next on the list of desirable features is the ability to translate from one input (or output) character to another. Normal ASCII characters such as upper and lower case A-Z, the digits 0 through 9, and common special characters such as pound (#) or percent (%) are usually no problem for any communications system.

A problem arises for *control characters* that are usually not displayable, but cause certain actions. An *escape character* might be used to stop the current network action such as listing a message for example. The escape character might not ordinarily be generated from the keyboard of the microcomputer; defining a simultaneous press of the *SHIFT* and *up arrow* keys as *escape* or a similar definition would be desirable. In the best terminal programs all keyboard characters can be redefined for both input and output, and one key may even generate strings of characters.

Buffering the Data

In the dumb terminal program, text was displayed on the microcomputer screen as it came in. The data is lost after it has been displayed. Buffering the data not only displays the text on the screen, but simultaneously stores it in RAM (random-access memory). The "smart" terminal programs would have various commands to handle this buffering of data. A *reset* would start accumulation of data at the beginning of the RAM buffer. A warning message would be displayed when the RAM buffer space was running out. Typical RAM buffers would be 16,000 characters (bytes) in length.

Printing the Data

This feature allows the incoming and outgoing data to be simultaneously printed on the system printer of the user. Optionally, the contents of the RAM buffer could be printed at any time.

Disk Interface

One of the most desirable features in a "smart" terminal program is the ability to save incoming data as a disk file. Stock market information might be permanently saved on disk for later retrieval for example. Most terminal programs do this from the RAM buffer on user command. At a certain point in the accumulation of data, the user interrupts the terminal program, specifies a file name, and *dumps* the data to disk. A more desirable action is to define the file initially and then have the terminal program automatically save the data as a disk file. This is not always possible due to the *protocol* of the network and the architecture of the computer system, however. The network must be able to recognize the break in transmission while the terminal program of the user activates the disk; an alternative approach is simultaneous disk and RS-232C activity, not possible on all small computers.

A "smart" terminal program should not only be able to save incoming data on disk, it should be able to transmit a disk file to the other system, so called *up loading* of programs or data. (*Down loading* is reception of programs of data; again, these terms are dependent upon which system is the "main" system.)

Unfortunately, there is no standardization of program format or even data formats. What has been discussed up to this point has been primarily ASCII data—displayable and printable text characters with some embedded *control codes* that may be translated to system actions. In all fairness, to expect a terminal program to handle all types of program formats is unrealistic. Apple program files are completely different from IBM program files, for example, and could not be easily up- or down-loaded.

What a smart terminal program might be able to do, however, is to up- or down-load program files in ASCII (or even in non-ASCII) for the *same* small computer. Ideally, for example, it should be possible to transfer a BASIC program for the TRS-80 Model I from one system to another. The "smart" terminal program should provide the proper prompts and menus for the actions.

Editing and Filtering of Data

We are now getting into features that are not exactly necessary, but are nice to have. One of these is *filtering* of incoming characters. You might look on filtering as a combination of translation and rejection of incoming characters. The incoming data is automatically tested by the terminal program for certain special characters. These characters are then discarded or translated by the system.

Editing features allow you to search an existing file for certain characters and to delete or translate them to other characters or strings of characters. You might, for example, have to delete all top of form characters that would cause your system line printer or display to start a new page, but would confuse the network.

Screen Formatting

Certain terminal programs allow you to format the data as it is received to fit your display parameters. If your display is only capable of a 32-character display line, for example, the "smart" terminal program might reformat incoming data so that it is arranged neatly on the screen.

Menus and User Interaction

Lastly, a "smart" terminal program should be *menu driven*. It should be geared to easy use by the system user. The program should be interruptible at any time and should display system functions in a menu of items. System functions should be selectable with proper operator prompts so that you may initiate actions easily. And, needless to say, documentation should be adequate; unfortunately, this last criterion is almost never met in current terminal programs. Data communications are confusing to the neophyte and experienced user alike, and terminal program documentation is woefully inadequate.

STAND-ALONE TERMINAL PROGRAMS VERSUS OPERATING SYSTEMS

There are two ways in which to add a smart terminal program to your system.

If you have a cassette-based microcomputer, then you must buy a *stand-alone* "smart" terminal program that operates without interaction to any system software or with minimum interaction. In some cases the stand-alone terminal program will also interface to disk operating system(s) available for the microcomputer. Expect to pay around $40 to $100 for the package.

If you have a disk-based system, it may be possible to get a "smart" terminal program free, as part of the operating system software. As a matter of fact, the latter approach is probably desirable on many microcomputers because the operating system and "smart" terminal software will work together as an integrated package, with the operating system taking care of such things as filtering, translation, and printer output, and the terminal program providing the *mainline* functions. Here, the price of the terminal program is bundled in the cost of the operating system, which may run $100 to $200.

MODEMS ARE GETTING SMARTER, TOO

Another aspect of computing that has changed dramatically in several years is the modem. Early modems were generally acoustic couplers that connected to the computer via rubber cups that held the telephone headset. The early acoustic couplers for microcomputers are being replaced by true modems without the *acoustic coupler* portion at excellent prices. These plug directly into the phone line, and replace or supplement the telephone. (It's still hard to shout, "Is your system still functioning?" over a pure modem.)

The newer modems contain a microprocessor and are "smart" modems. Following are some of the features found on a typical modem of this type, the DC Hayes Smartmodem.

Dial-Up Capability

Older modems had to be manually connected to a network. With some modems, however, the modem will automatically dial a number! This means that you may leave your computer running with your system clock keeping time, and at a predefined time automatically dial a network or another computer. The modem will dial either in a touch-tone or pulsed dial mode and will even wait for a second dial tone (as through a PBX board) before dialing the number.

Combined with a simple program, you can have unlimited dial-up capability, as you may define any number of numbers for your computer to dial. A short command string of characters precedes the number to be dialed, which is also a string of ASCII digits.

Auto-Answer Capability

The modem will also automatically answer the phone. A command string defines the number of rings before the answer and other parameters. This capability means that you can implement your own network to run unattended without operator intervention (with the addition of available network software)!

Other Features

The auto-dial and auto-answer features are the most impressive functions of the Hayes modem. The modem also provides every possible function found in earlier modems, however, and many more besides, all generally defined by strings of command sequences that are output to the modem. Some of the additional features are

- Definition of data, start, stop, parity
- 0-300 baud data rates
- 40-character command buffer
- Audio monitor on modem
- Amateur radio capability for radio teletype (RTTY)

- Automatic disconnect
- Speed of dialing programmable
- Carriage return definition
- Redial capability

There are several other smart modems available at this time, and there will undoubtedly be more in the future. Expect to see as many features implemented in the modems as the manufacturers' marketing departments can think of, and that can be controlled by the self-contained microprocessor. Prices for modems of this type are on the order of $250.

PHILOSOPHICAL QUESTION II: WHICH IS SMARTER, THE COMPUTER SYSTEM OR THE USER?

Data communications and networks have not yet realized their true potential at this point. There has been a lot of hoopla about them, but many users are somewhat intimidated by their complexities. The "smart" terminal program and modem are two types of products that make data communications a lot easier and introduce many new users to the benefits of network information retrieval. Both the smart software and smart hardware will get even smarter in the future, so you'd best start boning up on data communications before you're outpaced by a computer and your own computer at that!

Teaching Your System To Talk and Listen

I wonder how many of you have seen the "Star Trek" episode in which Scotty, the chief engineer of the U.S.S. Enterprise, is talking to the ship's computer.

"Ship's Computer, give me a rrrrepair time estimate for the warrrrp drrrrives . . ."

"Unable to match rrrrepair . . . unable to match warrrrp . . . unable to match drrrrives . . .," the computer replies in mechanical tones.

"I dinna ken yourr rrrresponse!"
"Unable to match dinna . . . unable to ...."

Current speech recognition equipment is even in worse straits than the equipment on the Enterprise. On the other hand, speech *synthesis*, the black art of producing computerized speech, is getting better and better. In this chapter let us look at some of the techniques and equipment for speech recognition and synthesis, and answer the questions: "Can a small computer really talk?" and "Can a small computer really listen?"

THREE WAYS TO REPRODUCE A VOICE

To understand some of the equipment being offered for computerized speech, we have to examine some of the basic approaches to speech synthesis. There are three common techniques being used today—*digitized speech, format speech,* and *linear predictive coding.*

Digitized Speech

The simplest of these is digitized speech. This is also called *pulse code modulation.* It operates as shown in Fig. 15-1. Speech appears as an irregular waveform, as shown in the figure. The range of frequencies for the human voice extends over the range of human hearing, but the most important of these are the lower frequencies up to about 6,000 cycles per second, or 6,000 *hertz.* (The term *hertz* is another way of saying cycles per second.)

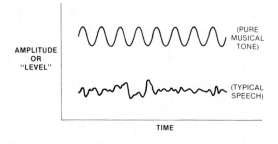

Fig. 15-1. Typical speech waveform.

This frequency range covers the range of tones comparable to those produced by a piano keyboard. Of course, a voice is made up of many frequencies together, hence, the irregular shaped waveform, rather than a smooth *sine wave* of a pure musical tone.

Any audio waveform can be *digitized* by a device called an *analog-to-digital converter.* The adc converts the different levels of the waveform to digital values that can be held in a computer. A complementary device, called a *digital-to-analog converter,* or *dac,* converts the digital values back to analog levels.

Some small computers have built-in adc's and dac's; others require simple, inexpensive options to provide these functions. If

176

your computer has a *joystick*, for example, it will have an adc to convert the joystick position to computer readable digital position; if your computer plays music, chances are it has a dac to reproduce the musical tones.

To convert an audio waveform to digital form, the adc takes samples at regular intervals thousands of times per second and stores the resulting digital values in RAM memory. To reconvert the digital values to an audio waveform, the dac changes these digital values back to discrete levels. Typically, a dac can only generate 64 different levels or so, and the resulting output resembles the input but is made up of *steps*, as shown in Fig. 15-2.

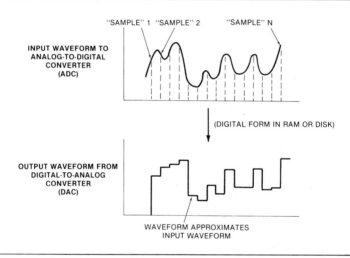

Fig. 15-2. Converting a waveform to digital form.

To record speech with this method, a program reads in the data from the adc and stores it in RAM or on disk. To play back the speech, the digitized data is sent to the dac and small audio amplifier.

The advantage of this approach is that the voice quality is excellent; it sounds almost identical to the original. The disadvantage is serious: Because thousands of samples must be taken every second (typically twice the highest frequency required), RAM memory and disk space is used up very rapidly. In this brute force approach the RAM is used without modification; one second worth of speech will require about 6,000 bytes of storage! This means that the typical microcomputer can hold about 3 seconds worth of speech in RAM or 25 seconds worth on diskette.

This digitization method can be modified, however, to compress the data. Dead time at the beginning and end of words can be discarded, and special compression techniques can reduce the number of bits required for each digitized value to ½ or ¼ of the number by brute force digitization.

Variations of the digitization method sample the audio waveform more crudely and produce fewer digital levels and/or approximate the waveform by triangular waves. The result is generally lower quality voice with higher storage capability.

There are various products for small computers that use this technique; some computers record onto disk and let the digitized data be edited. For any of you who are experimenters, *Byte* and similar magazines have many construction articles that use this technique.*

Phoneme and Formant Synthesis

A second type of voice synthesis has been around since the early days of microcomputers in 1975. It is generally called *phoneme synthesis* but is more correctly called *formant synthesis*.

Formants are natural resonances of the human vocal tract, such as the hissing sounds that Apple owners make towards TRS-80 owners or that TRS-80 owners make towards Apple owners, or that IBM owners make towards both. Phonemes are the basic sounds of the English language, such as the "ouuu" sound in "zoo," or the "tch" sound in "touch." The phoneme method of voice synthesis defines every phoneme (about 64) by a series of values that can be output to special hardware. The special hardware is an electronic emulation of the human vocal tract, with

*See the following article: William Barden, Jr., "Voice Synthesis for the Color Computer," *BYTE*, February, 1982.

circuitry to produce the individual sounds of the vocal tract. When combined together, the resulting sound is similar to the phoneme. When phonemes are strung together, words can be created. The word "pin," for example, would consist of the phoneme for "phh," followed by the phoneme for the "ihh" sound, followed by the phoneme for the "nnn" sound.

You have probably all heard this phoneme method of generating speech. It is the classic science-fiction speech sound—a mechanical sounding voice with no inflections at the end of words or sentences and a regular cadence.

This speech synthesis method produces speech that is the least understandable of any technique, but it does have one advantage—it uses minimal memory to store the parameters. Speech can be generated by data rates of 10 bytes per second or so, compared to thousands of bytes per second for digitized techniques. This means that a 150K diskette could now hold 30K words or so.

Of course, in addition to the poor quality of this speech there is another disadvantage. The user must string together the phonemes to create words. This can be very time consuming and frustrating, even though "shorthand" programming techniques, such as using character strings in BASIC, can be employed.

An example of a speech synthesis unit using this technique is the Radio Shack TRS-80 Voice Synthesizer, which sells for about $400. Other units are available for other small computers.

(What the Heck Is . . .) Linear Predictive Coding

The third popular type of voice synthesis is *linear predictive coding* (LPC). Don't let the name scare you. It operates in a combination of digitized and phoneme techniques. Voice samples are first digitized. They are then "number crunched" by a very large computer. Parameters of the voice are determined by the computer and then used as inputs to vocal tract electronics (all of the electronics is on a chip, of course). Human speech analysts smooth over and enhance the voices by changing the parameters.

LPC sounds very good. Not as good as the best digitization, but much, much better than the phoneme method. More importantly, the data required to make up a second of speech is on the order of 2,000 bits per second, or 250 bytes per second. A 150K byte floppy disk could hold about 3,000 words or so.

LPC is used in Texas Instrument chips for the TI-99 personal computer, and similar approaches are used in other semiconductor manufacturers' voice synthesis chip sets. Expect to see more equipment that uses this technique in small computers.

THE FUTURE OF VOICE SYNTHESIS

Microcomputer products for voice synthesis, thus far, have been disappointing. However, a great deal of work is being done in this area by semiconductor manufacturers such as Texas Instruments, National Semiconductor, General Instrument, and others. Combinations of the above techniques are producing prepackaged, synthesized speech that sounds excellent and requires only a hundred bytes of storage per second of speech. Expect to see add-ons for microcomputers with vocabularies of hundreds of words costing on the order of a few hundred dollars shortly. By the mid 1980s, digitized speech output for tens of thousands of words will probably be available for large systems, and there will be a corresponding "trickle down" to less expensive equipment for microcomputers.

SCOTTY REPROGRAMS THE SHIP'S COMPUTER

Back to the voice recognition part of this chapter. It is much easier for a computer to synthesize speech than to recognize speech patterns. Here is how a typical voice recognition unit recognizes speech. The incoming waveform is made up of a number of frequencies, as we discussed earlier. The speech is processed by filter hardware to separate the frequencies into 16 groups. The waveform is repeatedly sampled, typically 50 to 100 times per second.

The patterns of frequencies obtained from the input speech are then aligned. This involves determining the beginning and ending of the word and dividing the total speech input into "time slices" of equal duration.

The resulting pattern can now be compared to a set of patterns stored in memory. These are typically accumulated during a learning phase. The closest match for the pattern is found from the set of patterns. If the characteristics of the pattern differ too greatly from the closest pattern, or if two sets of patterns that approximate the input pattern are found, the input word is designated as no match, just as the ship's computer did with Scotty.

There has not been a great deal of computer hardware devoted to word recognition up to this point. Word recognition is considerably less than expected. I remember attending one computer show where a voice recognition unit was being demonstrated. The unit was to identify the word being spoken from a table of words and repeat it via voice synthesis.

"One," said the human operator.

"Two," said the computer.

"Two," said the human operator.

"One," said the computer.

And so on . . .

One of the problems in voice recognition is related to *speaker independence*. Voice recognition equipment can be programmed to recognize one voice but will not recognize another voice saying the same word. If you can accept the fact that your computer will recognize only your voice, fine, but there are other problems.

If you alter your voice, as during times of stress, the voice recognition will probably falter. Another problem is the ability of voice recognition equipment being able to detect word endings. The speaker may have to pause after every word. A third problem is the size of the vocabulary that the equipment can recognize; recognition of several dozen words is a far cry from automatically typing a manuscript from verbal input.

Again, we have to look to the current work in progress for larger systems. In the last part of 1981, speech recognizers costing $3,500 to $65,000 had error rates of 2% to 8% for male and female subjects.

The question is, can you tolerate such an error rate for small computer input? I don't think so, when you consider that a 5% error rate is about one word out of 20 misrecognized, as this sentence indicates. I certainly wouldn't want such a voice recognition unit on the nearby San Onofre nuclear reactor.

Again, much work is being done in the area, but it appears that quality voice recognition is going to lag voice synthesis by ten years or so, and that reasonable small computer equipment will be still further behind.

"Unlock That Door You Overgrown Calculator!" — Computer Control of Your Home

Computers adjust coolant temperatures in nuclear reactors, count the number of bottles of lo-cal soda that come through assembly lines, weigh logs at lumber mills, and read price information at supermarkets. Surely, they can easily adjust your home air conditioning, control your lawn sprinklers so that they water only when required, and act as efficient burglar alarms. Can't they? In general, the answer at this point in microcomputer technology is a No! that echoes from the upstairs guest bedroom to the basement workshop of my heavily mortgaged abode. In this chapter let us look at some of the ways of connecting the "real world" to computers, some of the problems involved in using computers in the home, and forecast the future for computer home control.

HOW DOES THE COMPUTER TALK TO THE EXTERNAL WORLD?

Before we discuss some of the problems involved in using a small computer for control purposes, let us review how most microcomputers communicate with the external world. We have talked about many of these *interfaces* in previous chapters, but here is a recap. These channels to and from a computer are shown in Fig. 16-1.

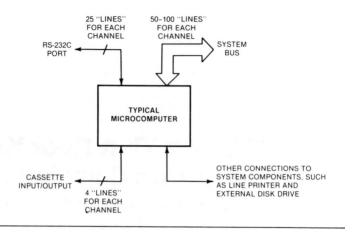

Fig. 16-1. Microcomputer external-world connections.

RS-232C Communications Interface

All small computers, and large ones too, have a standardized *interface* to the outside world called the RS-232C port. This is usually an option with the computer and typically costs about $100.

The RS-232C port usually consists of a 25-pin connector that connects to a ribbon cable for line printers, telephone modems, plotters, or other devices that are designed to communicate with a computer system by using the standard RS-232C signals.

The RS-232C interface is a standard way of connecting computer and other equipment together, and many devices are designed to connect to RS-232C ports. When manufacturers design a new piece of hardware to be used on a computer system, their first thought is to design it to interface to an RS-232C port.

Computer System Bus

A second type of interface is the computer system bus connector. The computer bus is a set of standardized signals established by the computer system manufacturer. Many times they are related to the signals used by the microprocessor in the microcomputer.

The system bus may be anywhere from about 50 lines (represented by pins on the connector) to 100 lines. If you look for the largest connector on the back of your computer, chances are that it is the system bus connector. On some systems such as the TI-99 or Radio Shack Color Computer, the system bus connector is the same connector used for plugging in a ROM pack. On a few systems, there are special card slots that have system bus signals and are designed specifically to accept logic boards for special-purpose hardware; the Apple II and IBM Personal Computer are examples of small computers that have a number of empty slots.

Generally, the system bus is not standardized among many manufacturers. An IBM Personal Computer system bus will be radically different from an Apple II system bus, for example.

One exception to this is the S-100 bus, a standardized bus used on many microcomputers (many of which are no longer manufactured). A plethora of manufacturers produce cards that plug into the standardized connectors of the S-100 bus.

Another exception to this is the IEEE bus used on the Commodore computers. This is an industry standard bus designed primarily for electronics test equipment.

The system bus is another way of connecting external devices to a small computer system and chances are that you will find a few manufacturers of special equipment that have designed their equipment to plug into the system bus for your computer.

Other Interfaces

The RS-232C port and system bus are the most popular ways of connecting external equipment to a small computer. Depending upon your system, however, there are a number of other ways to connect external devices.

Most small computers have a cassette port so that a small cassette tape recorder can be used to store BASIC and other types of programs. It is possible to use the cassette port to connect simple external devices to the computer system, and some manufacturers have designed equipment to do so.

Another *interface* to a small computer is through the line printer connector. Many small computers, including the Radio Shack Model I, Model II, and Model III, use a standardized line printer "bus" called the Centronics bus (after the line printer manufacturer who established it). It is possible to hook up an external device to this line printer bus by proper design.

There are other connectors that you will find on the back of your system, such as disk drive connectors, but the interfaces above are the most common.

USING THE INTERFACES FOR REAL-TIME CONTROL

Now that we know what types of interfaces are on a typical small computer, what can we do with them? Basically, four types of control operations can be done with the computer interfaces: discrete output, discrete input, analog input, and analog output.

Discrete Lines

The term *discrete output* or *discrete input* means that a single control signal may be sent out or read by the computer. A line is a single output or input.

Discrete output from the computer turns a light on or off, turns a valve on or off, turns an air conditioner on or off, dials a telephone by a series of on/off pulses, or performs some other on/off action.

Discrete input to the computer reads the on/off status of a burglar alarm switch, reads the on/off status of a smoke detector, or senses a dark/light condition.

Discrete inputs and outputs are relatively easy to implement on a microcomputer. Various small manufacturers provide a number of devices that have a number of discrete line inputs and outputs, typically 8, 16, or 24 lines. Often this interface is provided in the form of a parallel input/output board that plugs into an existing card slot. Other times the interface is a parallel-serial board that combines both discrete line output and RS-232C type interfaces. A typical configuration is shown in Fig. 16-2.

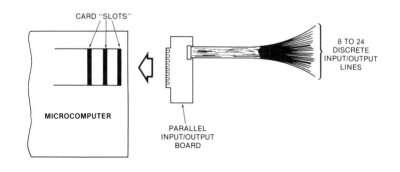

Fig. 16-2. Typical input/output board.

The parallel input/output device may attach to the system RS-232C port but often attaches to the system bus. In some cases even the cassette port is used for a single on/off line.

The typical cost for a parallel I/O controller is between $100 and $200. Programming of such a device is usually very simple and can be done with BASIC by a single command or at least only a few simple commands.

The problems of such a controller, however, are not in the implementation of the device—they are in attaching the lines to real world devices.

Given an on/off output at your home computer, how do you utilize it to turn on your electric lawn sprinklers? There are a number of problems. One problem is conversion of the weak signal on the discrete line to a more powerful controlling signal, such as the 24-volt ac signal required to operate a lawn sprinkler valve. Along with this problem is the related problem of isolating deadly power line voltages from computer equipment and humans.

Another significant problem is that of running lines around the house or property. It is fine to think in theoretical terms of using a home computer to control sprinklers and lights but another to string 12 pairs of heavy duty wires from the computer location.

One solution to the problems above is BSR system controller. The BSR controller operates through existing wiring to turn any light or electrical outlet off or on, or even to dim lights. It is an elegant, compact solution to discrete line output. Several companies offer a microcomputer interface to the BSR controller so that your home computer can be used as a master controller and timer.

Aside from the BSR controller, however, there are few devices that will provide long-distance control of devices in the home and solve the problems of stringing wires, conversion of the control signals, and electrical isolation. The design effort should not be all that complicated. Perhaps we will see more devices of this type with the proliferation of home computers.

How about the input of on/off signals from remote locations? Here again, the problems are not all that profound. Devices can be made that send an on/off signal over long distances reliably where the signal may be read in by a parallel input controller. Such a device should only cost a few dollars per unit. Again, there are no current devices that will do this, with the exception of a few small manufacturers. Even the BSR controller is no help here, as it operates only as an output device, sending on/off signals to remote locations but not accepting inputs.

The only current solution for the small computer users who wants to monitor remote devices for on/off conditions is to fabricate their own if they are conversant with elementary electronics. This would involve buying a parallel input/output board if it is available for your system, running the necessary wires, designing some rudimentary switch-type monitors, and writing the necessary program to monitor the inputs. All of these steps are achievable, but to say that it is an easy task would be misrepresenting the facts. Parallel input/output boards are available for the Apple II, IBM Personal Computer, and TRS-80 computers, among others.

Analog Inputs and Outputs

The discrete inputs and outputs we have been discussing are relatively easy to implement (in spite of the lack of equipment) and easy to program. However, many things we would like to use our computer to monitor and control in our home are not on/off conditions but are a variety of values. Temperature is not on or off, for example, but a range of values that cover hundreds of degrees.

Wind speed, humidity, room lighting, current flow, and water pressure are all examples of the real-world physical quantities that could be measured by a home computer. In some cases, we also want to output a range of values, as in the case of controlling motor speed, but these are in the minority, so we will just consider *analog inputs* in this discussion.

What is involved in using a home computer to measure these physical quantities? As you might guess, this problem is an order of magnitude more complex than discrete inputs. The general scheme is shown in Fig. 16-3.

The real-world quantity is first converted to an electrical *analog* quantity by a *transducer*. The transducer produces an electrical voltage that can be measured by an analog-to-digital converter or adc. The adc sends the digital form of the value to the microcomputer over the system bus lines.

This type of operation is in widespread use throughout industrial applications of computers. Why haven't we seen the same types of equipment in home computers?

One reason is simply cost. Transducers that convert temperature, water pressure, or rotational speed into electrical form are expensive, usually hundreds of dollars. However, here is the interesting part. One of the reasons for the expense is that the transducer manufacturer goes to great pains to make the device *linear;* this means that twice the water pressure would result in twice the voltage or other electrical parameter. However, computers can easily work with *nonlinear transducers*. This should spawn a variety of less expensive transducers but has not up to this point.

A second reason that we have not seen devices to read in analog values is that the electronic circuitry is more complex for the adc

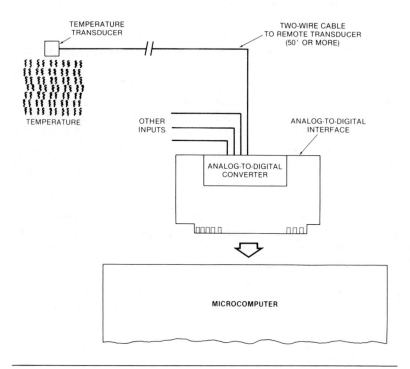

Fig. 16-3. Measuring analog inputs.

interface. The adc itself is inexpensive (on the order of $10 or so), but the device by its nature is best connected to the system bus, which requires additional semiconductor logic.

Another problem with the analog input is that it is easy to monitor one input, such as temperature from one room, but it is more difficult to connect many inputs to the computer. A number of inputs must be selected one at a time, or *multiplexed*, and this requires additional logic and increases the cost of the interface.

Finally, there is the same problem of wiring. It is simply not very feasible to string wires from 23 different transducers to the central computer point. What is really required is a BSR-type controller for real-world analog inputs via existing power lines, and this is not yet available.

What are available are special-purpose interfaces for the most popular microcomputers, generally from the smaller manufacturers. For example, one computer manufacturer makes a dual thermometer interface for a small computer. The interface consists of a computer plug-in board and remote temperature probes. Temperature can be measured over -55 to $+125$ degrees C and stored on disk or printed. The unit is about $260.00.

You will find other special purpose interfaces of this type from other manufacturers.

OTHER PROBLEMS IN HOME CONTROL

All the above problems could be solved fairly easily if there were a market for control of the home through small computers. However, there are some additional problems to think about.

First of all, any computer controlling the home must be dedicated to the task full time. If you sit down at the keyboard and start entering a BASIC program, the program that is monitoring your heater and solar energy unit will be suspended. It is possible in larger systems to have a high priority or foreground task while running a low priority or background task, but most small computers do not allow this sophistication. Currently then, you must have a dedicated, full-time computer system executing a home control program. Perhaps in the future we will see more operating system software that can run both foreground and background tasks at the same time.

It goes without saying that if you are controlling such home functions as heating, air conditioning, and burglar alarms that you must have a reliable system. My opinion, and I believe that this could be backed up with a great deal of confirming documentation, is that small computer systems are simply not as reliable as individual controllers for these functions. The more sophisticated the device, the more chips that it uses; the more chips that are used, the greater the likelihood that the device will fail. When the computer system fails, by the way, there is no redundancy as there would be in commercial control systems. Your home would be down until your computer could be repaired.

Along these same lines, think about the success of the stand-alone BSR system, the model that does not require a computer. It is easy to use and does not require a person conversant with small computers. It seems reasonable that the successful control systems will be individual "idiot-proof" units that are not geared to computing systems, are not as sophisticated as small computers, and will have mass-market appeal. We may see an integrated home-control computer, but it will probably not be an adaptation of our small computers with control circuitry.

And that is the current status of computers that control the home. We are a long way from achieving the goal, and yet the technology is there. If we are lucky, you may wake up in 1985 to a pleasant computer voice that says, "Good morning! I've turned on the coffee pot and the central heating. Temperature outside is 20.2 degrees Celsius." If we're not so lucky, we may be forced to do it ourselves, after those six courses in electrical engineering!

Index

TO THE READER

Sams Computer books cover Fundamentals — Programming — Interfacing — Technology written to meet the needs of computer engineers, professionals, scientists, technicians, students, educators, business owners, personal computerists and home hobbyists.

*Our Tradition is to meet your needs
and in so doing we invite you to tell us what
your needs and interests are by completing
the following:*

1. I need books on the following topics:

_____

_____

_____

_____

_____

_____

2. I have the following Sams titles:

_____

_____

_____

_____

_____

_____

3. My occupation is:

_____ Scientist, Engineer	_____ D P Professional
_____ Personal computerist	_____ Business owner
_____ Technician, Serviceman	_____ Computer store owner
_____ Educator	_____ Home hobbyist
_____ Student	Other _____
	_____

Name (print) _____

Address _____

City _____ State _____ Zip _____

Mail to: **Howard W. Sams & Co., Inc.**
Marketing Dept. #CBS1/80
4300 W. 62nd St., P.O. Box 7092
Indianapolis, Indiana 46206

22008